Faculty Development

Faculty Development

Creating a Collaborative Culture in Community Colleges

Farrell Hoy Jenab and
Heidi L. Hallman

AMERICAN
ASSOCIATION OF
COMMUNITY
COLLEGES

ROWMAN & LITTLEFIELD
Lanham • Boulder • New York • London

Published by Rowman & Littlefield
An imprint of The Rowman & Littlefield Publishing Group, Inc.
4501 Forbes Boulevard, Suite 200, Lanham, Maryland 20706
www.rowman.com

86-90 Paul Street, London EC2A 4NE

British Library Cataloguing in Publication Information Available

Library of Congress Cataloging-in-Publication Data on File

ISBN: 978-1-4758-5907-2 (cloth : alk. Paper)
ISBN: 978-1-4758-5908-9 (pbk. : alk. Paper)
ISBN: 978-1-4758-5909-6 (electronic)

♾™ The paper used in this publication meets the minimum requirements
of American National Standard for Information Sciences—Permanence
of Paper for Printed Library Materials, ANSI/NISO Z39.48-1992.

This book is dedicated to faculty developers at community colleges and the faculty they support.

Contents

Preface

Though the mission of community colleges is focused on teaching, there are few books that examine how the culture of a community college might foster faculty engagement and collaboration. Faculty development, while a staple of four-year institutions (Beach et al., 2016), is still in the fledgling stage at community colleges. Faculty developers—or directors and faculty who lead initiatives around teaching—can be found at community colleges, yet many community colleges still do not have personnel directly tied to faculty development. This book highlights the affordances of faculty development at two-year colleges.

Through case studies developed before and during the COVID-19 pandemic, this book also grapples with what types of faculty development benefit faculty. Describing the benefits of the scholarship of teaching and learning (SoTL) and faculty learning communities (FLCs), the book delves into how faculty developers fostered these initiatives within their community college contexts. Moreover, faculty developers detail the benefits that SoTL and FLCs brought to faculty and how these initiatives became part of a changing culture at their institutions.

Midway through this book project, the COVID-19 pandemic created waves for all involved in higher education. The study that this book was premised on aimed to outline how faculty developers fostered collaboration among their community college faculty; however, the COVID-19 pandemic presented a very real reason why collaboration became important and necessary. Therefore, instead of only focusing on long-term faculty development initiatives such as SoTL and FLCs, this book pivoted and also addressed how faculty developers responded to the sudden changes in course teaching and delivery brought about by the pandemic. If authentic collaboration was not present on college campuses pre-pandemic, the pandemic era pushed all involved in higher education to seek greater synergy from collaborative efforts. The whole now became more important than the parts and new possibilities arose during the challenging COVID-19 era.

This book makes a unique contribution to the literature on faculty engagement within the community college context. It discusses two very different eras—faculty development pre-pandemic and faculty development during the pandemic. Through the voices of faculty developers, we see the possibilities for the future. Contrary to a limited view of faculty development within the community college context, this book views faculty developers as catalysts for changing their institution's views about teaching and professional learning. And faculty developers can be in a position to steer institutional change around teaching and learning.

Acknowledgments

We would like to thank the faculty developers who so willingly gave their time and expertise by allowing us to interview them. Zoom interviews with these individuals took place in two distinct eras— the "before times" and the "pandemic times." Interviews that took place in the "before times" seem to us now to have taken place long ago. However, as we analyzed our findings, we saw how faculty development had sustained many of its core tenets, even throughout the challenges of the pandemic era. Effective faculty development, as we discuss throughout this book, is founded on collaboration and, in many ways, collaborative realities only increased during the pandemic era. At the outset of this book project, we had no idea that we would live through an era of so much change but also so much innovation. We hope that the things we have learned have only strengthened our understanding of teaching today.

Farrell would like to thank Johnson County Community College, particularly for the opportunity to collaborate with a faculty so dedicated to excellent and innovative teaching. She also thanks the faculty in the doctoral program at the University of Kansas School of Education and Human Sciences for guiding her in laying the groundwork for this research. Above all, she thanks her family and friends for their love and encouragement.

Heidi would like to thank the University of Kansas School of Education and Human Sciences, especially noting how the research support program fostered by the school helped support this project. In addition to the support that the University of Kansas offered, Heidi wishes to thank her husband, John Mattes, and her children, Ari, Helena, Sigrid, and Nico, for offering her unyielding support throughout her years as a faculty member at the University of Kansas.

Chapter One

Faculty Development in Community Colleges

Challenges and Opportunities

In 2018–2019, more than 1,400 community colleges existed in the United States that served just over eight million students from a wide variety of backgrounds (Teachers College Columbia University, n.d.; U.S. Department of Education, 2017). Over the past several decades, community colleges' open access policies have drawn in both traditional and nontraditional students for vocational training as well as preparation for future transfer to four-year institutions.

Literature chronicling the evolution of community colleges in the United States (e.g., Brint & Karabel, 1989; Cohen & Brawer, 2003; Rhoads & Valadez, 1996) has underscored that although community colleges have steadily provided more access to education for many students, completion rates for students who attend community colleges (i.e., the attainment of a certificate, associate's, or bachelor's degree) remain a critical piece of assessing how well community colleges are preparing their students for their futures. Teaching and teachers at community colleges are critical to fulfilling the mission to assist students in successfully completing programs at community colleges.

Providing open, affordable access to education, then, is the main task of community colleges, and the primary job of its faculty is to teach (Twombly & Townsend, 2008). As teaching is core to the community college mission, many continue to consider the quality of teaching at community colleges. Faculty developers, those who coordinate teaching initiatives and facilitate instructors' access to both development of teaching skills as well as the technologies involved in teaching, are becoming a critical part of making teaching at community colleges successful. Faculty development, the ongoing professional learning of faculty members, has become more widespread in the past two decades across all types of college campuses (Austin & Sorcinelli, 2013).

This book focuses on teaching's primary role in U.S. community colleges by outlining how faculty developers and faculty development can bolster the mission of teaching. Within higher education—both at community colleges and four-year institutions—faculty developers are often viewed as the professionals who lead changes related to teaching. Effective faculty development is premised on the idea that instructors can learn and grow as teachers, therefore better serving their students. This book examines faculty development in the community college context to consider how we might continue to foster high-quality teaching for all students.

TEACHING: CONTENT AND PEDAGOGY

Teaching is a complex act that requires knowledge of both content and pedagogy, and faculty development must focus on both. Faculty developers, a rather new group of professionals within community colleges, are often tasked with creating programs for faculty that span the disciplines, urging them to inquire into their practice and thereby improve student learning through improved teaching.

To provide some background about teaching at community colleges, it is important to first understand that community college faculty members are expected to have expertise in their discipline but are not expected to research or publish within the discipline, as are their university counterparts. Rather, they are judged "on the strength of their ability to help students learn and to engage students with different backgrounds, ethnicities, and aspirations" (Shannon & Smith, 2006, p. 15). Community college faculty are highly qualified scholars, and if their professional setting does not require them to pursue research within their discipline, it is expected that they turn their professional skills toward learning and enacting the best, most effective means of teaching their subject matter.

Though faculty within the community college context are experts in their own subject matter, they often have less knowledge of the theory and practice of successful teaching models and techniques (typically known as pedagogy) for enhancing student learning and engagement (Burns, 2017). Many instructors who teach at community colleges are hired with limited prior teaching experience, and only 16% of instructors at community colleges were found to have prior K–12 teaching experience (Gahn & Twombly, 2001).

Community college faculty, then, while trained to be disciplinary researchers and experts, have not necessarily been trained to instruct others in these disciplines (Eddy, 2010). Instead, faculty, for the most part, have learned to teach through an apprenticeship model; essentially, they have learned to teach through thinking about and replicating the ways that they were taught. Until recently, this lineage of apprenticeship has remained uninterrupted, and faculty have continued to lecture, review, test, and assume this is the only pedagogical model rigorous enough for higher education.

This book addresses how faculty developers address changes and challenges in teaching within the community college context. As teaching models have evolved, central themes that this book addresses include the role of collaboration in faculty development and what supports exist within the community college context to support faculty in their continual development as teachers.

In the remainder of this chapter, a description of the mission of teaching within the community college context is articulated. Next, the chapter explores the roles of faculty developers and faculty development within the community college context. Finally, this chapter presents an overview of traditional frameworks for faculty development, including the scholarship of teaching and learning

(SoTL) and faculty learning communities (FLCs), as well as an overview of the book's chapters.

THE COMMUNITY COLLEGE CONTEXT

Since its beginnings in the early twentieth century, the community college has had a unique position in higher education. Its open-door policy makes it, in some ways, like a K–12 school, but it is still a postsecondary institution. Community colleges, originally known as junior colleges, were conceived as high-school based programs with vocational education, teacher education, and some general postsecondary coursework (Cohen & Brawer, 2003). Cohen and Brawer (2003) write that universities could have accommodated additional students, but a movement to remove freshman and sophomore coursework from universities continued to bolster the existence of community colleges.

Scholars have written rich and detailed descriptions about how community colleges have changed throughout their history (e.g., Cohen & Brawer, 2003; Robinson-Neal, 2009). One of the key features of the community college, its open access to all, has had unintended consequences in the eyes of some researchers. Brint and Karabel (1989), for example, have asserted that the community college has accentuated rather than mitigated social inequality as lower-income students were diverted to two-year community colleges from four-year institutions.

Murray (2002) believes that the mission of the community college is broader than that of four-year institutions: Community colleges are meant to serve a larger and more diverse group of students. Cohen and Brawer (2003) add to this discussion by characterizing the debate about community colleges a bit differently, emphasizing that individuals from all social classes must have opportunities to further their education and that the community college provides this opportunity. Finally, Levin & Montero-Hernandez (2009) note that students who attend community colleges are a distinct population—

oftentimes demographically, socially, and economically different from students at four-year institutions.

Though historically community colleges have served traditional students, who in their freshman year are seventeen to nineteen years old, recent years have shown a greater diversity of students, including nontraditional students who are adults with full-time or part-time jobs, live off campus, and seek specific job training (Cohen & Brawer, 2003; Hankin & Gardner, 1996). These descriptions of students contribute to better understanding the distinct student population that the community college serves.

Despite this recognition about their student population, community colleges are still viewed as "underperforming" by some, and stigmas about being a community college student exist (Michael, 2020). Narrow conceptions of community colleges miss a broader discussion about what the goals of community colleges might be—that goals include a large array of outcomes, including self-understanding, career goals, academic and vocational competencies, and increased skills and cognition. This broader picture must continue to be part of the discussion about the goals of community colleges. A broadened view of the mission of community colleges is better able to capture the intersections between institutional goals and students' goals and identities.

THE MISSION OF TEACHING WITHIN COMMUNITY COLLEGES

There are several seminal books that focus on teaching within community colleges that have shaped what is known about teaching within this context. One of these books, O'Banion's (1997) *A Learning College for the 21st Century* (1997), is premised on the idea that it is best for community colleges to reject *teaching pedagogy* and instead adopt *learning pedagogy*. Indeed, the book resonates with what Sorcinelli, Austin, Eddy, and Beach (2006) name as the era of higher education characterized by *The Age of the Learner*. The

1990s, as Sorcinelli et al. (2006) write, were filled with "new developments, fast-moving fields, and the complex, ever-changing dynamics of college teaching" (p. 9). As a result, faculty development programs were asked to anticipate and support new priorities, some of which included technology, multiculturalism, and assessment.

Another book, *Honored but Invisible: An Inside Look at Teaching in Community Colleges*, by Grubb and Associates (1999) emerged as a response to what Grubb et al. describe as a plethora of information about how faculty ought to teach but little evidence of what actual teaching looks like within community colleges. The authors of this text observed 257 classes at 32 community colleges in 11 states. Some findings from their study included that faculty follow a wild variety of practices because they lack institutional support. They wrote that, as a result, "under these conditions, the community college fails to live up to its promise as a teaching institution" (Grubb et al., 1999, p. 95).

Finally, in *Community College Faculty: At Work in the New Economy*, Levin, Kater, and Wagoner (2006) explore how to tie together community colleges' mission, students and faculty, and economy. Levin et al. (2006) conducted a case study of community college faculty to understand faculty behaviors in the areas in which they work. Levin et al. (2006) argue that globalization and managerialism have compromised the work and professional lives of community college faculty members. We know that, in the fifteen years since this book was written, the emphasis on managerialism and efficiency has only intensified.

Before this book moves into a discussion of faculty development and teaching at community colleges, it is important to define *teaching*. Teaching, as it is understood in relationship to the work of teachers, is rooted in Boyer's discussion of teaching as scholarship, something this book explores more in-depth in chapter 2. To Boyer (1990), teaching and scholarship about teaching must be intertwined. Scholarship not only applies to research, but also to teaching. Teaching, therefore, *transmits*, *transforms*, and *extends* knowledge (Boyer, 1990, pp. 15–24, emphasis added). As this book considers how multifaceted teaching is and how faculty developers can promote an environment that improves teaching, it is also necessary to consider who the teachers who teach in community colleges are.

WHO ARE FACULTY WHO TEACH AT COMMUNITY COLLEGES?

The majority of faculty at community colleges are part-time faculty (CCCSE, 2014). Full-time faculty at community colleges, unlike the full-time faculty at college and universities, spend the majority of their time teaching. A heavy emphasis on teaching has benefits and drawbacks. For example, it allows faculty to prioritize the teaching mission and spend their time and effort there. Yet, less time is available to pursue scholarship.

In order to begin a discussion of faculty professional development in the community college context, it is essential to outline the distinct features of teaching within the community college context. The first distinct feature to note is that faculty at community colleges generally have heavy teaching loads. At most community colleges, the teaching load is five three-credit courses per term, or fifteen credits per term (MLA, n.d.). Faculty may also teach four or five different course preparations, and although teaching is the primary job of faculty, they must advise students, serve on departmental and institutional communities, participate in division duties and professional development, and engage in community service (Levin, 2013).

A second distinct feature of faculty who teach at community colleges is that they have the highest percentage of tenured female faculty (Everett, 2011). There are many possible reasons for this, one being that perhaps fewer women earn doctorates, required for teaching at four-year institutions, and another being that community colleges may be perceived as more female-friendly, allowing more of a work–life balance.

Finally, another distinct feature of faculty who teach at community colleges is that the percentage of part-time faculty (adjuncts) is high. The Center for Community College Student Engagement (CCCSE) reports that part-time faculty teach about half of the courses offered at community colleges (CCCSE, 2014). Within the community college context, the use of adjunct faculty (also referred to as part-time or contingent faculty) helps control costs since this group of faculty is paid less and receives few or no benefits. Adjuncts are also hired on an "as needed" basis, so they have no guarantee of continued employment.

These distinct features of adjunct faculty at community college are also the most controversial. Adjunct pay at institutions of higher education is known to be low, and few institutions offer benefits for adjuncts (Adamowicz, 2007; Levin, 2013). In recent years, increasing attention has been paid to both how adjuncts provide institutions with low costs and flexibility and how adjuncts themselves have little loyalty to particular institutions because of the low pay, minimal benefits, and absent job security (Adamowicz, 2007; Jacoby, 2005; Schmidt, 2008). Some recent studies (e.g., Du, 2019) have sought to understand how use of part-time faculty may even influence students' career paths.

Though the above portrait of community college faculty presents a broad picture of who these faculty are, Twombly and Townsend (2008) write that not much more is known about community college faculty. The authors present several reasons why there may be a lack of knowledge about community college faculty, including that research designed for publication is "primarily conducted by individuals at research universities as part of their quest for tenure, promotion, or merit pay" (p. 8). The authors note that scholars tend to focus on what they know; in this case, the world of four-year institutions.

Other times, research about community college faculty appears as part of a general study of the professoriate in the United States. Therefore, no differentiation is made between faculty at community colleges and those at four-year institutions. Or there may be a direct comparison between the two groups of faculty (see works such as

Schuster and Finkelstein's *The American Faculty: The Restructuring of Academic Work and Careers*, 2006).

Also, of note is that research on faculty at community colleges likely appears in journals devoted to this group of faculty and the specific context of the community college. Twombly and Townsend (2008) argue that in general, journals devoted to higher education feature far less research on community colleges and the faculty who work there than journals specifically geared toward the community college context.

FACULTY DEVELOPMENT AND FACULTY DEVELOPERS IN COMMUNITY COLLEGES

The discussion of teaching in the community college context is undergirded by the recognition that, as of the 1970s, the student population in higher education was increasingly comprised of more first-generation, underrepresented, minority, nontraditional, and low-income students who required a different style of teaching than the traditional lecture (Gaff, 1975; Murray, 2002). While the student population at colleges was changing, the faculty was not. In the 1970s the concept of the adjunct instructor had not yet appeared and faculty tended to remain in their teaching positions for many years (Gaff, 1975). The combination of an unchanging faculty and a changing student population prompted the concept of *developing* existing faculty.

Gaff (1975) noted that faculty development could, as a concept, challenge the quality of colleagues' work. Historically, the idea of professional learning in higher education had revolved around the idea of sabbaticals, meetings of professional organizations, and institutional support for research. But Gaff also knew that scholarly competence did not equal teaching effectiveness.

Gaff studied over two hundred promising faculty development programs and found that there was no one-size-fits-all approach for effective instruction. Though Gaff wrote about faculty professional development over forty years ago, he identified three main approaches of improving instruction. The first, faculty development, specifically looks at how instructors acquire the knowledge and skills related to teaching and learning. The next approach, instructional development, focuses on improving student learning through new material, curriculum redesign, and systematic instruction. The third approach, organizational development, focuses on the larger institutional environment through improved team functioning and the creation of policies to support effective teaching and learning. The first strand of Gaff's approach to effective instruction, faculty development, is the work of this book.

HISTORY OF FACULTY DEVELOPMENT

The need for continual learning within any profession is critical. Yet, the role of faculty professional development (sometimes referred to as faculty professional learning) within higher education has not yet been solidified across all disciplines (Austin & Sorcinelli, 2013). In fact, most literature on faculty professional development in higher education can be found within journals about teaching, and professional development across community colleges and four-year institutions of higher education is often inconsistent and unevenly implemented across programs (Beach et al., 2016).

There is less research on professional learning and faculty development in the community college context than their is on faculty professional development at four-year colleges. While we draw upon research about faculty professional learning in four-year institutions to anchor our discussion throughout this book, we recognize that there may be distinct differences in what faculty professional learning may look like in the community college context as compared to the four-year college context.

Likewise, literature about faculty developers within the community college context is limited. The literature that does exist is quite critical of faculty development programs for being ad hoc, lacking in institutional support, and having powerless coordinators (Grant & Keim, 2002; Murray, 2001). Yet, this limited research is somewhat dated and new approaches to faculty development have been slow to be documented. This book hopes to feature some of these recent innovations.

Faculty developers are often catalysts for change at their respective institutions. Grupp and Little (2019) use the metaphor of a lever to describe the work of faculty developers. But the lever, as the authors describe, always depends upon the position of the fulcrum, dictating "how easily the lever pivots, what effort or load is required, and how efficiently or effectively the lever works" (Grupp & Little, 2019, pp. 3–4). So, faculty developers often have opportunities to initiate and direct change within their institution but must continuously assess how to access and propel change.

Distinct eras have shaped institutions of higher education and have bearing on how change may be operationalized by faculty developers. Sorcinelli et al.'s (2006) study of faculty development focuses on tracing specific eras of faculty learning; thus, their work can assist in identifying why faculty development has been on the rise in the past few decades. Specifically, the authors discuss how, beginning in the 2000s, the "age of the networker" came into being. For example, this era recognizes faculty development as an opportunity to address and respond to certain challenges in higher education. These responses both require and enable faculty across institutional disciplinary divides to work together for the betterment of the campus as a whole, allowing faculty development to become a collaborative and networked approach.

Today, we continue seeing the influence of the "age of the networker," but as Beach et al. (2016) describe, we are now responding to a context that the authors call the "age of evidence," an era shaped by increased accountability and data and influenced by heightened stakeholder interest in educational outcomes. The authors write, "faculty developers are being called on to support the needs of individual faculty members and their institutions in investigating and document-ing student learning" (p. 12). They are also being called on to address the needs of full-time faculty as well as part-time, non-tenure-track, and adjunct faculty.

As chapter 4 of this book illuminates, we may have entered a new era beyond the "age of Evidence" (Beach et al., 2016), one shaped by the COVID-19 pandemic. Higher education finds itself facing new realities. A disruption in teaching and learning, precipitated by the "first full pandemic year" (Alexander, 2020), has elicited questions about the best ways to teach students. As it is a time of uncertainty, the current era has mandated that traditional campuses reevaluate what the college experience is if it does not include the on-campus experience that it did before the pandemic.

What Are Characteristics of Faculty Developers?

Many faculty developers (42%) who administer faculty develop-ment programs in higher education hold their terminal degree in some area of education, allowing them to provide training in tra-ditional education theory and methodology (Beach et al., 2016). Over half of faculty developers are coming to the field from a more focused disciplinary background: 13% from STEM fields, 17% from the arts and humanities, and 27% from the social and behavioral sci-ences (Beach et al., 2016).

Faculty developers are almost always straddling roles in their institutions. Over half hold dual positions as faculty and administra-tors (Beach et al., 2016), and this trend has proven consistent for at least the last decade (Sorcinelli et al., 2006). This dual role allows faculty developers to provide leadership and administer programs while they keep a foot in the classroom. No doubt the continuation in a faculty role provides legitimacy and insight into the work they do supporting other faculty.

Faculty developers must inhabit a separate skill set to success-fully oversee a center for teaching and learning (CTL), yet many community colleges do not have a CTL. With a sole faculty development director, Community colleges often have a single faculty development director, and rely on that single individual to provide programmatic support around teaching to a wide variety of faculty members. Faculty developers must also act as personnel supervisors, being mindful of making sure staff do not become overwhelmed and that they have space to create projects that are personally and professionally meaningful (Cook, 2011).

Faculty developers must serve as liaisons between administration and faculty, actively identifying and aligning professional learning programming to any new initiatives identified by administration. they must also safeguard the reputation of teaching by upholding high standards for professional learning programs (Cook-Sather et al., 2019). Since the majority of faculty developers were faculty first, they often lack experience and training in these administrative roles. In the general higher education context, approximately 90% of faculty developers identify as white (Winkelmes, 2011). Because a major trend in faculty development is inclusive teaching practices, it is important to consider how this extreme underrepresentation impacts the design, focus, and success of these programs.

Statistics about faculty developers pertain to all higher education contexts; it is much more difficult to find information about faculty developers in the community college context. Shaffer's (2011) study of faculty developers at community colleges conveys differences in how faculty developers perceive themselves and their roles within their institutional context, and Shaffer articulates the ambiguous role that many faculty developers perceive they hold when they work within the community college context.

In response to the lack of understanding of faculty developers' roles within community colleges, this book aims to provide an understanding of faculty developers' work across different types of community colleges. It also aims to contrast faculty development before COVID-19 shaped the educational landscape with how COVID-19 shaped decision-making at community colleges during the pandemic.

OVERVIEW OF CHAPTERS

Though the mission of community colleges is focused on teaching, there are few books that examine how community colleges might foster greater faculty engagement with teaching. Faculty development, while a staple of four-year institutions (Beach et al., 2016) is still at an early stage at community colleges. This book makes a unique contribution to the literature on faculty engagement in teaching within the community college context.

Chapter 2, "Collaboration Through Faculty Development in the Community College Context," stresses how collaboration can improve faculty development. The chapter presents an overview of two core structures that facilitate faculty development at community colleges: the scholarship of teaching and learning (SoTL) and faculty learning communities (FLCs). SoTL supports inquiry and assessment of teaching in higher education, while FLCs not only create opportunities to conduct this inquiry and assessment, but also help build community and cultivate collaboration. Many of the tenets of SoTL and FLCs are referenced by the faculty developers featured in the book.

Using multiple case studies based on semi-structured interviews, document analysis, focus groups, and surveys, chapter 3 takes a holistic, in-depth look at faculty development within community colleges. The case studies of community colleges featured in chapter 3 were conducted before the COVID-19 pandemic and investigations were premised on the integration of the scholarship of teaching and learning (SoTL) and faculty learning communities (FLCs). Noting that these structures guide faculty development, SoTL and FLCs were viewed as pillars of faculty development that fostered collaboration among both faculty and administration as well as across disciplines. Discussing the challenges and opportunities they faced, the faculty developers who featured in chapter 3 help readers understand what incentives exist for faculty to participate in faculty development initiatives.

Chapter 4 features three case studies of community colleges based on observations during the COVID-19 pandemic. In these cases, the reader will see how faculty development shifted from long-term, sustained initiatives such as SOTL and FLCs to just-in-time (JiT) faculty development, as well as virtual and collaborative faculty development. The faculty developers featured in chapter 4 describe the challenges their colleges faced due to COVID-19 and how responding to them became a form of faculty development in and of itself.

Additionally, chapter 4 features the results of a survey conducted at one institution that highlights how faculty felt they were supported during the COVID-19 pandemic. Data from the survey depicts themes that affected students, faculty, curriculum, and assessment. Chapter 4 poses questions about how preexisting structures like SoTL and FLCs may be altered as a result of the pandemic era and outlines new initiatives faculty developers promoted during the pandemic era.

The final chapter, chapter 5, "Working Toward Collaboration in Faculty Development: Learning from Challenges," synthesizes the findings from faculty developers and faculty who were featured in chapters 3 and 4. Despite guiding faculty in two distinct eras—both before and during the pandemic—the chapter discusses similarities across the two eras in how faculty developers enhanced purposeful collaboration across faculty, disciplines, and departments. In both eras, fostering a culture that supported improved teaching was the primary goal of faculty developers. Additionally, the final chapter discusses how faculty developers solved problems alongside faculty concerning a host of issues during the pandemic. Faculty developers focused on just-in-time (JiT) faculty development and virtual collaboration.

The case studies presented in this book strive to present the work of faculty developers at community colleges. This portrait, across two different eras, will prompt faculty developers to consider the value of in-depth and long-term initiatives such as SoTL and FLCs, while balancing these initiatives with imperatives such as student-centered pedagogy and just-in-time faculty development. Using the tenets of collaboration as a unifying lens, the book promotes interdisciplinary and collaborative processes that focus on how faculty developers can continue to promote faculty professional development within their institutions. By featuring innovations of the COVID-19 era, this book also fosters a reflection on how faculty development must respond to changing contexts.

Chapter Two

Collaboration Through Faculty Development in the Community College Context

This chapter unites the various structures and practices of faculty development by honing in on the importance of collaboration within the community college context. First, the chapter grounds and describes two structures for faculty professional development, the scholarship of teaching and learning (SoTL) and faculty learning communities (FLCs). The chapter begins by situating faculty professional development within community colleges and then describes the benefits that SoTL and FLCs can have within a professional development model.

Next, collaboration theory is discussed as the theory that undergirds faculty professional development within the community college context. Finally, the exploration of collaboration theory sets the stage for discussion of how faculty development has had to pivot in an era shaped by uncertainty. As the COVID-19 era has shaped faculty developers' work, this book grapples with what features of faculty development have remained the same and which have shifted. Through case studies featured in chapters 3 and 4, the book aims to respond to the following question:

How do faculty developers in the community college context promote collaborative professional learning experiences for faculty?

As noted, the concept of collaboration unites the case studies featured across chapters 3 and 4. Next, this chapter describes faculty professional learning more generally, and then discusses SoTL and FLCs.

CONSTRUCTS FOR PROFESSIONAL LEARNING FOR FACULTY AT COMMUNITY COLLEGES

Professional learning for faculty in higher education can take many forms. One organization devoted to the study of professional learning in higher education is the Professional and Organizational Development Network in Higher Education (POD Network), formed in 1976 at the conference of the American Association for Higher Education (AAHE). The POD Network was the first organization to focus entirely on promoting the work of Centers for Teaching and Learning (CTLs). At the time of the POD Network's inception, Mary Lynn Crow, the POD Network's first executive director, urged higher education institutions to reorient its focus to teaching and learning (as opposed to research and scholarship). While this resonates within the four-year research university context, community colleges, whose mission has always focused on teaching, must also be included in this vision.

In this chapter, the forms of faculty professional development that best support the work of faculty who teach in community colleges are considered. Specifically, the chapter outlines tenets of two key structures that promote faculty development: the scholarship of teaching and learning (SoTL) and faculty learning communities (FLCs). The chapter explores how these structures have supported the mission of teaching within community colleges.

This chapter also considers how collaboration might operate within a culture changed by the pandemic. How does collaboration shift when faculty development is premised on faculty's immediate needs rather than their distinct interests for inquiry? As the COVID-19 pandemic changed course delivery to mostly online formats in community colleges across the United States, this chapter considers shifts in collaboration in a changed environment. Can faculty developers still draw upon faculty-led initiatives amidst such change?

Hallmarks of effective faculty professional development in both the K–12 (Darling-Hammond et al., 2009) and higher education sectors (Beach et al., 2016; Condon et al., 2016) emphasize that features of effective faculty development must point to its sustained and cohesive nature, as such qualities lead faculty to prioritize and operationalize improved student outcomes, including retention and performance (Condon et al., 2016; Elliott & Oliver, 2016). Through prioritizing sustained and cohesive faculty development, the creation of a culture of growth for both students and faculty is fostered. Sustained and cohesive faculty development builds a cycle in which faculty invest in their teaching and collaborate with others. Faculty development opportunities, then, become a space where changes in one's teaching are valued.

In the study of faculty development conducted by Beach et al. (2016), the scholarship of teaching and learning (SoTL) and faculty learning communities (FLCs) were viewed as methods to add to or expand upon by research universities, comprehensive universities, and liberal arts colleges. While the scholarship of teaching and learning (SoTL) and faculty learning communities (FLCs) have gained momentum for years at four-year universities, progress at the community college has been slower.

Little is written about SoTL or FLCs in the community college context and there are few models for implementing these structures for faculty professional development at the community college level (Ford & Peaslee, 2018). The next section introduces these structures and makes a case for their implementation at community colleges.

PRINCIPLES OF THE SCHOLARSHIP OF TEACHING AND LEARNING (SoTL)

The scholarship of teaching and learning (SoTL) has emerged as a practice that supports inquiry and assessment of teaching in higher education. SoTL can be defined as "the systematic study of teaching and/or learning and the public sharing and review of such work through presentations, performance, or publications" (Poole & Simmons, 2013, p. 39). By its very nature, SoTL promotes collaboration because the shared results are expected to be applicable across disciplines (McCarthy, 2008, p. 7).

SoTL's interdisciplinary approach is significant to fostering faculty development in teaching because, in addition to a general lack of teaching expertise, faculty members and departments at the community college are known to be isolated within departments and even from each other. Such "siloing" (or isolation from other departments and disciplines) in higher education can lead to a culture resistant to transformational change and growth (Lloyd, 2016).

On the other hand, organizations that foster a collaborative, cross-disciplinary culture, including institutions of higher education, also enhance professionalism and growth (Varagona et al., 2017). Faculty learning communities (FLCs) have emerged from the principles of SoTL as a means for faculty to build community while assessing their own teaching effectiveness and sharing their results with others (Burns, 2017).

Fostering such a collaborative, high-quality teaching culture is of particular relevance at community colleges, where student demographics range widely and teaching is the primary role of faculty members. According to a report written by Baldwin and Chang (2014) for the American Association of Community Colleges (AACC), for community colleges to continue to fulfill their mission of providing affordable, accessible education in the face of rapid cultural and economic changes taking place in society, collaboration at entirely new levels, among internal and external entities, will be essential. To serve their students effectively, community college faculty benefit from increased collaboration across, among, and within disciplines.

Although the related concepts of *action research* and *professional learning communities* are well established in the K–12 professional development world, the use of SoTL and FLCs in higher education—especially at community colleges—is a relatively new, but growing area, and faculty learning communities are emerging at colleges and universities all over the world (King & Lonnquist, 1992). Some institutions have been implementing SoTL and FLCs for up to three decades while others are in the beginning stages. Proponents and implementers of these strategies are eager to share their knowledge and experience.

Community college instructors are well positioned to become leaders and innovators in both the implementation of the SoTL and FLCs. Community college faculty are rigorously trained in their disciplines and have entered a professional setting, the community college, where teaching their subject matter is the primary focus of their job. Yet, faculty at community colleges "rarely have the opportunities to share their pedagogical work with others" (Latz, 2012, p. 4). The SoTL movement is an opportunity for community college faculty to emerge as leading scholars in the field of teaching excellence in higher education.

Unfortunately, in spite of the emphasis on teaching in the community college context, instructors tend to lack innovation and effectiveness in their teaching (Burns, 2017). Like most teachers in higher education, they have little training in pedagogy or andragogy, but instead have had an emphasis on their discipline or subject (Miller-Young et al., 2018).

Community college faculty members have limited opportunities to consult or collaborate with each other, and instructors design their courses individually, often relying on trial-and-error methods and unsystematically evaluating their effectiveness through personal reflection (Worthy, 2016). Integrating SoTL principles into the community college setting could potentially transform the role of community college faculty within the academy, to become "experts knowledgeable in the complex processes of teaching diverse students" (Burns, 2017, p. 154).

Sperling (2003) discusses implementation of SoTL at the community college level, noting that "this new 'scholarship' encourages faculty to understand themselves both as practitioners who can utilize research to enhance practice and researchers who can contribute to their profession through significant practice-based research" (p. 593). SoTL represents a paradigm shift through which community college faculty members (and their institutions) can view their role within the academy as to create a dynamic connection between pedagogical/andragogical research and on-the-ground classroom teaching.

Because SoTL requires researchers to share and make public the results of changes to their teaching, this paradigm shift will require an expansion and reconceptualization of the community college mission to support externally oriented scholarship. Community college faculty members might have the expertise and experience to study questions about their teaching, but they would need institutional, cultural, and ideological support to conduct research and share the results of their findings with their colleagues at colleges and universities (Worthy, 2016).

Community college faculty and administrators need not limit their professional participation to serving on boards of academic organizations and publications focused only on the community college; they can be included in those organizations and publications focused on all undergraduate teaching in higher education. Through the principles of SoTL, community colleges could potentially play an influential role in improving teaching effectiveness at all levels of higher education.

HISTORY OF SoTL

SoTL originates with Boyer's (1990) work, which classified the scholarly activities associated with SoTL into four categories: discovery (traditionally what the academy labels "research"), integration (making connections across disciplines), application or engagement (making teaching publicly available for other scholars), and teaching. Boyer further identified three teaching approaches: effective teaching, scholarly teaching, and the scholarship of teaching and learning. Shulman (2000) later defined effective teaching as any teaching that results in student learning, a scholarly grounding in a specific field, and "that which occurs when our work as teachers becomes public, peer-reviewed, and critiqued, and exchanged with other members of our professional communities" (Miller et al., 2004, pp. 31–32).

There are compelling reasons for the implementation of SoTL across higher education institutions. Draeger (2013) argued that SoTL helps students learn more effectively and gives teachers the tools they need to share their disciplinary expertise. It also offers instructors opportunities for professional and intellectual growth, building interdisciplinary communities that invigorate intellectual capital. SoTL not only enhances the institution's policy making, it "embodies a spirit of pedagogical innovation that enlivens the quest for learning and reminds us why it is worth pursuing" (Draeger, 2013, p. 6).

Cassard and Sloboda (2014) offered a model for supporting the shift to a new paradigm that promotes SoTL and fosters faculty and administrative buy-in. They suggest that if colleges and universities create a strong and focused research agenda using SoTL, they will be in a position to provide assessments of student learning and evidence of learning outcomes that are more and more in demand from stakeholders.

Hatch (2005) argues for integrating SoTL into the classroom. Teaching is often solitary and quite personal, and it's not unusual for educators to feel reluctant to have their peers observe or judge them; yet, the profession suffers when teachers are not collaborative and open to sharing with each other. Making teaching more public within a collaborative environment could generate a culture that fosters the SoTL. Hatch (2005) offers five recommendations to create more open communication, information sharing, and collegiality:

1. documenting and representing what teachers actually do in the classroom;
2. establishing new forums for the presentation, publication, and review of teachers' work;

3. creating an audience for teachers' work and building the collective capacity to interpret and assess what goes on in the classroom;
4. implementing standards that recognize and encourage teachers' professionalism; and,
5. developing new standards that support federal mandates for improving teaching quality.

Others, like Felten (2013), operationalize these collaborative efforts within SoTL itself. Felton (2013) works to distill the myriad forms and methods of SoTL into five guiding principles. These principles define the ideal SoTL as providing: "1) inquiry into student learning, 2) grounded in context, 3) methodologically sound, 4) conducted in partnership with students, and 5) appropriately public" (p. 121). Taken as guideposts, these five principles appropriately guide individual SoTL inquiries as well as larger SoTL initiatives. Therefore, these guideposts can serve to "clarify and demystify SoTL to those who evaluate this work" (p. 124). On many campuses, there is still skepticism, however, about a claim that there can truly be a "scholarship" of teaching (Felten et al., 2007).

PRINCIPLES OF FACULTY
LEARNING COMMUNITIES (FLCs)

Faculty Learning Communities (FLCs) go hand-in-hand with SoTL, and this chapter now moves to trace the roots of FLCs, providing some essential history and details on how FLCs have been implemented.

Cox (2004) established the widely accepted definition and protocol for a faculty learning community within the parameters of SoTL:

> a cross-disciplinary faculty and staff group of six to fifteen members (eight to twelve members is the recommended size) who engage in an active, collaborative, yearlong program with a curriculum about en-

hancing teaching and learning and with frequent seminars and activities that provide learning, development, the scholarship of teaching, and community building. (p. 8)

The aims of FLCs resonate with John Dewey's ideas about learning in communities that are student-centered (Dewey, 1933). Principles that emphasize learning in communities aim to be successfully transferred to faculty through FLCs, and faculty, like students, are positioned as inquirers.

FLCs can be either cohort-based (focusing on a particular group of faculty and staff) or topic-based (focused on a specific teaching need or issue). The curriculum for FLCs is more "structured and intensive" than in more traditional faculty groups, such as learning circles or brown bag discussions (Cox, 2004, p. 9). Participants are expected to explore deeply and assess the outcomes of their topics.

FLCs are proven to be effective for varied purposes. Bond (2015) describes the benefits of offering FLCs to non-tenure-track faculty, whereas Gordon and Foutz (2015) used FLCs to explore the most effective ways to conduct their campus-wide first-year seminars. At a university in the United Arab Emirates, Engin and Atkinson (2015) report the model worked effectively to support curriculum changes.

Research has shown that FLCs are useful in STEM teaching and learning (Elliot et al., 2016; Smith et al., 2008). A case-study conducted by Schlitz et al. (2009) describes how their FLC fostered a "culture of assessment" on their campus, and Becket et al. (2012) used an FLC to reflect on and implement service-learning goals. Notably, FLCs are proven to be effective in fostering collaboration. FLCs can help overcome "pedagogical solitude" (Tovar et al., 2015) and participants in one study (Schlitz et al., 2009) described how the energy level and focus of a well-run FLC can increase motivation and engagement.

Cox (2016) notes that FLCs benefit junior and senior faculty members alike, as they "offer participants time, safety, funds and colleagueship across different disciplines in order to reflect on past teaching and life experiences and chart new directions" (p. 73). FLCs

have been implemented across different institutions, sometimes varying year-to-year based on budgetary or administrative directives.

Regardless of the stated purpose for FLCs, one consistent outcome of most FLCs appears to be enhanced collaboration, whether
through a campus-wide policy change, an increase in collaboration
among participating colleagues, or even an institutional cultural
shift. Thus, a more formal examination of the effects of FLCs on
collaboration is useful for those wishing to foster a collaborative
environment in higher education. Understanding the nature of collaboration itself is an important part of this process.

UNIFYING SoTL AND FLCs
THROUGH COLLABORATION THEORY

Because the principles of SoTL and FLCs require public sharing
and cross-disciplinary collaboration, collaboration theory (Wood
& Gray, 1991) became an appropriate and apt framework for
examining both SoTL and FLCs' effects on college teaching and
culture. Understanding how collaboration works is enigmatic and
difficult to quantify, and many researchers have sought to formulate a pragmatic theory of collaboration. Wood and Gray (1991)
shaped a theory of collaboration and analyzed nine research-based
studies that addressed several theoretical perspectives on the collaboration process.

Wood and Gray's (1991) work identifies theoretical questions,
and, in answering these questions, develops an understanding of the
"process" component of collaboration. The authors' first effort to
develop a theory of collaboration was to develop a definition for the
phenomenon of collaboration. After comparing and analyzing the
different ways collaboration was defined, Wood and Gray (1991)
integrated them into the following definition:

> Collaboration occurs when a group of autonomous stakeholders of
> a problem domain engage in an interactive process, using shared

rules, norms, and structures, to act or decide on issues related to that domain. (p. 146)

The authors also define and clarify another element of the theory, the role of the *convener* in a collaborative process. The convener establishes and guides the collaboration, but questions remain about how the convener gains and uses the authority to do so, whether through legitimation, facilitation, mandate, or persuasion. The authors also address "environmental complexity" (p. 155) and the role it plays in collaboration. Most organizations seek to reduce uncertainty and turmoil, yet collaboration tends to increase complexity within organizations, therefore also increasing the turbulence in an organization's environment.

The exchange of knowledge and information that can occur through collaboration fosters an enriched appreciation of the problem and can result in a kind of synergistic form of problem-solving within organizations. Wood and Gray (1991) argue that the potential for participants in collaboration to receive a benefit, whether individually or as a group, makes collaboration possible, but questions remain about the relationship between self-interests and collective interests.

Collaboration theory has touched organizations and altered the ways in which organizations understand their collaborative processes. Gajda (2004), for example, developed the Strategic Alliance Formative Assessment Rubric (SAFAR) to help organizations "quantitatively and qualitatively self-assess" the strength of their collaborative efforts (p. 76). The rubric draws from five principles of collaboration theory: "(1) collaboration is imperative . . . (2) collaboration is known by many names . . . (3) collaboration is a journey and not a destination . . . (4) with collaboration the personal is as important as the procedural . . .and (5) collaboration develops in stages" (pp. 67–69). Such efforts provide a deeper explanation of the processes that shape collaboration.

Other scholars build on Wood and Gray's (1991) work, but take slightly different approaches. Using a grounded approach to collaboration theory, Colbry et al. (2014) move from seeking to understand the interorganizational or intergroup level to the interpersonal level, identifying six causal themes in collaboration: turn-taking, observing or doing, building group cohesion, influencing others, organizing work, and status seeking, which were further organized into two categories—individual first and team first.

Scholars have also sought to study not only how the individual participates in a collaborative environment, but also how the group operates. Given and Kelly (2016), for example, look beyond individual behaviors within a group and attempt to study "the collectivist, social nature of group activities" (p. 2). Given and Kelly studied the members of mentoring circles and found that the diverse demographic profile of the circles allowed for "diverse experiences and a broad range of information sharing opportunities beyond what individual members would typically encounter" (p. 9). The cohesive nature of the group, then, prompted members from a variety of backgrounds to collaborate effectively.

Bridging the divide between the practical and the theoretical, Thomson and Perry (2006) elaborate on the *black box* of collaboration, or the elusive unknowns about collaboration that are difficult to quantify. They recommend "looking inside the black box of collaboration processes [to] find a complex construct consisting of five variable dimensions" (p. 21). To collaborate effectively, the authors argue that it is necessary to understand five process-oriented dimensions of collaboration: the process of collaborative governing, the process of collaborative administration, the process of reconciling individual and collective interests, the process of forging mutually beneficial relationships, and the process of building social capital norms.

Thomson and Perry caution against "collaborating for collaboration's sake," or for individual gain, because, when paired with the "complexity of the collaboration process" (p. 28), this will likely result in failure. While this aspect of the interactive process of collaboration is least understood (hence the term *black box*), it is nonetheless necessary for facilitators and change agents to understand and apply the five dimensions of collaboration.

Finally, Stavrakis (2009) ventures more deeply into the theoretical dimensions of collaboration, and therefore attempts to bridge "the philosophical gap between modern and postmodern theories of understanding reality, knowledge, and social practice in the context of human collaboration and communication" (p. 16). Stavrakis points out that there is not a "complete body of knowledge or an ontological framework" to support either theoretical or methodological levels of collaborative practice" (p. 17); hence, it may be important to establish one.

Stavrakis also addresses the so-called *black box* of collaboration, and describes the actant's role within the collaborative process as the creative individual whose cognitive experiences are "influenced by bodily, biologically driven, senses, but are seen as black boxes and therefore we cannot speak of their true inner being" (p. 183). This irrational process can be associated with creativity, yet the creator is not able to explain that process.

COLLABORATION IN A TIME OF UNCERTAINTY

Though the case studies presented in chapter 3 detail how SoTL and FLCs have been operationalized by faculty developers, chapter 4 moves to characterize faculty development in an era of change. As we have passed through what is now referred to as the "first full pandemic year" (Alexander, 2020), COVID-19 has shaped the daily work of community college faculty from mid-spring 2020 to the present.

Chapter 4 presents cases of faculty developers' response to the pandemic era. While the hallmarks of sustained and coherent faculty development are still valued in the pandemic era, new circumstances have presented faculty developers with pressing dilemmas that need to be solved. Collaboration, surely, was present in this era as it was before the pandemic, but chapter 4 explores how collaboration in the pandemic era differed from the kinds of collaboration featured in chapter 3.

The literature on collaboration helps outline what one might look for in effective collaboration within the pandemic era. Wood and Gray's (1991) emphasis on the *convener* in collaboration is imperative when thinking about an era in which so many things have become decentralized due to a reliance on the virtual environment. As the case studies in chapter 4 illustrate, during the pandemic, in-person collaboration between faculty and faculty developers was no longer possible, for physical meetings—planned or not—were no longer possible. Throughout the first full pandemic year, the collaboration that unfolded did so in spontaneous and unexpected ways.

The pandemic era mandated change for community colleges across the United States, and all community colleges were faced with choices about how to navigate through the pandemic. Faculty within the community college context experienced a plethora of situations that altered teaching modalities, and even experienced shifting teaching modalities at different points throughout the pandemic. Faculty who had experience teaching online generally found the move to teaching in these new modalities (online, hybrid, or HyFlex) more seamless than those who had previously delivered all of their classes face-to-face. All faculty, though, found that teaching while adapting to digital technologies takes practice, time, and support.

Faculty who remained on campuses and continued to deliver in-person courses during the first full pandemic year also faced new realities. Masks and plexiglass screens, as well as socially distanced classrooms, became the new norms. Expression (voice and facial expressions) was impacted and affected faculty and students alike. During the first full pandemic year, who was able to choose what kind of teaching modality they would teach in also became a question. While some faculty were able to select which teaching modality they felt most comfortable teaching in, others, such as adjunct faculty, often had to be flexible in facing the realities of what they were asked to do.

The new teaching landscape ushered in by the pandemic prompted faculty developers to ask new questions about the tools faculty needed to adapt. Just-in-time (JiT) faculty learning, in place of an optional and inquiry-based structure, aided collaboration. JiT focuses on various faculty needs, including perceived needs and on-demand needs. Faculty developers learned to recognize that some faculty needed more on-demand faculty development related to online teaching at the beginning of the pandemic era. Presenting information to faculty in smaller chunks of learning became the JiT faculty development that faculty developers harnessed to promote collaboration.

Much like FLCs, virtual FLCs (VFLCs) became a way to connect disparate faculty members, a phenomenon that was already occurring before the pandemic but greatly intensified as a result of it. In a study of online teacher communities of practice, Hough et al. (2004) found that more successful online communities: "(a) have a more focused versus less focused purpose or problem base for discussions, (b) frame the directions for discussions and suggest to participants what kinds of discussions are expected, and (c) tend to support trust among the members through efforts to build community and encourage feelings of ownership" (p. 383). Though the pandemic mandated online virtual communities in some form, having a purpose or a problem base for discussion led pandemic-era faculty development to be more purposeful.

Due to their mandated nature, virtual communities of practice also had to become a space in which to build trust and community among community members. And to build trust, one must foster relationships. As chapter 4 illustrates, faculty developers' role during the pandemic era became increasingly encompassed by the social aspect of faculty development; faculty developers often found themselves devoted to fostering collaborative groups with the sole purpose of building community.

COLLABORATION AND FACULTY
DEVELOPMENT IN CONTEXT

Focusing on collaboration, both before and during the pandemic era, the following two chapters illustrate how faculty development unfolded across multiple contexts. Hearing from faculty developers about the structure of their community colleges allows readers to recognize the processes involved in collaboration. Thus, recognizing and examining individuals, recording interactions among individuals, identifying strong links between individuals, identifying adversaries and contributors, constructing a basic outline of the context, and recording connectivity and identifying possible purposes (Stavrakis, 2009) became priorities in analyzing faculty developers' work through the lens of collaboration theory.

Understanding collaboration within faculty development allows us to articulate how faculty development is a synergistic process through which the sum becomes greater than its parts. This can be a powerful force of change and growth within the community college context.

Next, in chapter 3, three cases of how faculty developers implemented SoTL and FLCs at their respective institutions are featured. As the chapter illustrates, the scholarship of teaching and learning (SoTL)—a structure that supports inquiry and assessment of teaching in higher education—and faculty learning communities (FLCs) not only create opportunities to conduct this inquiry and assessment, but also help build community and cultivate collaboration.

In the following chapter, the book moves into real-life community college contexts, exploring the roles and work of faculty developers with faculty. Through this exploration, it becomes clear how SoTL and FLCs, as well as the contexts and collaborations, worked together to create distinct possibilities for faculty learning.

Chapter Three

Case Studies of Faculty Developers at Community Colleges

Implementing the Scholarship of Teaching and Learning (SoTL) and Faculty Learning Communities

This chapter examines the cases of three different community colleges and the faculty developers leading faculty development initiatives at their institutions. Describing the ways that faculty developers have implemented SoTL practices and FLCs with their faculty, this chapter explores the ways in which the implementation of SoTL practices through FLCs promotes improved pedagogical practices as well as fosters collaboration. This chapter seeks, especially, to illustrate how this happens differently at each of the three institutions featured and keeps the book's guiding question at the forefront:

> How do faculty developers in the community college context promote collaborative professional learning experiences for faculty?

The book draws upon the case study (Creswell, 2007; Stake, 2000; Yin, 2014) as an appropriate methodology to explore faculty developers' work at community colleges, for, according to Yin (2014), case study is a research strategy that is useful in contexts that call for the "distinctive need . . . to understand complex social phenomena" in contemporary, real-world situations (p. 3). The three cases presented in this chapter were selected by the researchers as those that they wished to examine in-depth; they were also eventually considered to be part of a larger case that illustrates the integration of collaboration in faculty professional development across the community colleges featured.

INSTITUTIONS AND PARTICIPANTS

This chapter features cases that involved faculty development professionals who were implementing SoTL practices using Cox's (2004) model for faculty learning communities. The table below presents features of the three community colleges explored in this chapter. (All names of people and places discusses are pseudonyms.)

Table 3.1. Community Colleges Implementing the Scholarship of Teaching and Learning (SoTL)

Community College	Region of United States	Size of Institution and Distinguishing Features
Northern Lakes Community College	North	12,500 students, two campuses; faculty are unionized
Southern Pines Technical College	Southeast	20,000 students, six campuses; faculty are not unionized
Eastern Shores Community College	Northeast	10,000 students, two campuses; faculty are unionized

The data collected from participants from the three community college focused on the implementation of both the SoTL and FLCs. The following chapter, chapter 4, features three additional institutions; however, data from the institutions featured in chapter 4 were collected during the COVID-19 pandemic. As many scholars have started to document, the COVID-19 pandemic prompted many K–12 schools and institutions of higher education, including community colleges, to prioritize their most pressing needs and pivot in regard to how instruction was delivered. Chapter 4 intends to capture this so-called pivot but also asks what features of faculty development can be sustained in a new era of pressures and changes.

This chapter, in which data were collected before the COVID-19 pandemic, features three distinct contexts: Northern Lakes Community College, Eastern Shores Community College, and Southern Pines Technical College. Data collected from Northern Lakes Community College included interviews with two participants, a faculty member and an administrator. Melinda Reynolds, one participant, is a non-tenured instructor in the English department. She teaches two courses a semester, which is half her teaching load; she gets credit release for the other half so that she can coordinate the SoTL program. Sarah Carrington, the other participant, is the college's vice president of academic & student affairs. While Sarah does not have hands-on involvement in the SoTL program, she helped to initiate and implement the program, and is able to allocate funding for the project.

Josh Daniels is a full-time instructor in the Spanish department at Southern Pines Technical College, the second community college featured in this chapter. In his role as an instructor, Josh became involved with the institution's Teaching and Learning Center (TLC), and eventually took the job of coordinator there, which allowed him to have release time from teaching one class per semester. Recently, he took over as director of the TLC, which also allows one class release per semester.

Nancy Martinelli, from Eastern Shores Community College, is the final community college faculty member featured in this chapter. At Eastern Shores, Nancy is a full-time faculty member in the English department. She and a chemistry professor are co-coordinators of their SoTL program. Faculty at Eastern Shores have a five class per semester teaching load, and faculty who participate in SoTL receive "reassign time," which releases them from teaching two of their classes per semester.

DATA COLLECTION AND ANALYSIS

Data collection methods for the cases featured in this chapter included semi-structured interviews with the faculty developers described above. Interviews were followed by two focus groups involving small groups (three) of the participants (see protocols featured in Appendix A). As faculty developers, all participants had experience in facilitating SoTL and FLCs within their respective community colleges.

Interviews were conducted and recorded using Zoom, an online communication platform. Immediately after each interview, the interview content was transcribed verbatim. The faculty development professionals featured in this chapter represent community colleges from different regions of the United States: north, east, and southeast. This purposeful selection aimed to contrast not only the regions in which these schools were located but how faculty members were either unionized or not (see Table 3.1).

Each of these institutions was at varying stages of implementing programs in support of faculty development. Following individual interviews, participants joined a virtual focus group discussion via Zoom, which, was also transcribed verbatim afterward. Two focus groups were conducted, each with three participants. In addition to the interviews, the researchers reviewed copies of administrative documents relevant to the planning, implementation, and assessment of the SoTL initiatives at the respective institutions. The content of these documents was reviewed and coded in order to present relevant similarities, differences, and perspectives that may be unique to each specific institution.

Data from interviews with the participants was analyzed through establishing inductive codes. After data collection and thorough data immersion, in vivo and axial coding (Strauss & Corbin, 1990) was used to uncover themes that emerged from the the data. This "bottom-up" approach allowed themes to arise that focused the scope of the study and bounded the cases.

The analysis process also used deductive coding constructs. In taking a deductive approach to coding the data, themes were sought within the data that resonated with the literature on SoTL and FLCs, and faculty development more generally. The framework of collaboration theory (Thomson & Perry, 2006) offered a unifying lens from which to view the data. After inductive and deductive analyses were completed, cases were written that described faculty development in each of the three contexts.

Next, the chapter describes how faculty developers at the three different community colleges implemented SoTL and FLCs at their respective institutions. This part of the chapter features the voices of the professors and faculty development professionals from these institutions who were doing this work. First, each of the individual cases (Northern Lakes Community College, Southern Pines Technical College, and Eastern Shores Community College) are described; following that, an exploration of the themes that emerged from the data is explored.

IMPLEMENTING THE SoTL
AND FLCs WITH FACULTY

Northern Lakes Community College

Northern Lakes Community College is a two-campus college located in the northern United States. With an enrollment of approximately 7,800 students, it has approximately 300 full- and part-time faculty. Although the college does not have a formalized faculty development structure such as a Center for Teaching and Learning, Melinda, a full-time faculty member in the English department, and Sarah, an upper-level administrator, collaborate to offer professional development opportunities for their faculty. Originally calling this faculty development the Applied Research Initiative, Melinda and Sarah were looking for a way to encourage faculty members to examine their own teaching while also modeling research practices for their students.

To facilitate this, Melinda and Sarah looked for other community colleges offering similar programs, yet were unable to find any. It was then that they discovered that universities were already promoting this kind of research under the name of the scholarship of teaching and learning. The institution studied programs at several universities on which to model their own SoTL program, and in 2014 they offered their inaugural Scholars Program. A flyer promoting the program says that the Scholars Program "brings together faculty from across disciplines and experience to participate in a Scholarship of Teaching and Learning (SoTL) faculty learning community. [F]aculty are supported as they develop, implement, and present research results at a conference or in a journal."

The Scholars Program called for applicants who were "interested in improving the teaching and student learning experience." The five selected faculty members met for a one-day retreat in August, and then had monthly meetings to continue progress, share ideas, collaborate, and obtain consultation and support. The SoTL Scholars Program at Northern Lakes Community College is a two-year commitment, and participants receive a semester stipend as well as funding to attend a teaching and learning conference.

The program is administered by Melinda, a full-time faculty member who receives release time from two courses per semester to coordinate the program. When Melinda implemented the program, the concept of SoTL was new and not widely understood at Northern Lakes, but awareness of SoTL grew quickly, as the first two cohorts had completed the program and the application process for the third cohort had begun by the time of Melinda's interview. She noted that faculty interest was evident.

Applicants have about a month to apply, and typically ten or more faculty members apply for each of the cohorts, which have been limited to five members. "So, that's really good," said Melinda, "that we've had more people than spots available." This kind of interest in faculty development is significant as it is often difficult to elicit faculty participation and enthusiasm for professional development activities, particularly if there is not a strong supplementary financial incentive.

Sarah, the upper-level administrator involved in faculty development at Northern Lakes, believed that the way Northern Lakes promoted the program accounted for the interest from faculty. She said, "I think it's a partnership between administration and faculty."

She also tried to balance her role as an administrator with the role Melinda had as a faculty member when she noted: "I try to give Melinda the stage because I think it's received much better when it comes from full-time faculty. Faculty just don't want something that the administration is shoving down their throats."

Faculty perception of who or what is behind a faculty development initiative extends beyond who is offering it. Although the promotional flyer called for applicants to refer to the program as a faculty learning community, Melinda and Sarah later chose not to use that label broadly because of past faculty perceptions. Sarah said, "As an institution, we did student learning communities for a number of years. I think there might be, unfortunately, a negative connotation for some folks that would not necessarily be warranted, so we don't call them faculty learning communities." Despite the name change, the groups generally followed Cox's (2004) model. "We don't necessarily call it something specific other than [a] cohort, but this is a scholarly program," said Melinda.

The cohorts for faculty learning at Northern Lakes are selected with attention toward disciplinary diversity. "We have been really intentional about that," said Sarah. "We make sure that we're not just all the psychology department faculty, for example. We also have some occupational programs. We've had a number of physical therapist assistant faculty that have gone through the program." The diversity within the cohorts has fostered an observable effect on collaboration among faculty. Sarah noted that this makes them true "communities of practice . . . where they have those conversations to help strengthen one another."

Melinda and Sarah noted that five participants in a cohort was the ideal number of participants. They said that five members makes it so there are enough members to bring different levels of expertise and experience, but few enough members to make sure it is meaningful for everybody. Resources also play a part in the cohort's success, and Sarah noted that five members per cohort is the number that the institution is realistically financially able to sustain each year.

The first semester of the program is devoted to educating the participants about SoTL and helping them define their research question. By the end of the first semester, each participant is expected to submit a human subjects application to the college's institutional review board for approval. The program offers support from the college's Office of Institutional Research in developing and submitting a human subjects application. In addition, librarians assist participants with research for their literature reviews.

Because participants have different levels of experience doing academic research, "there's lots of conversation and lots of sharing," said Melinda. "Yes, it's redundant in a lot of sessions, because there's multiple places you have to repeat the same information, but it's very intentional in its purpose." The monthly meetings provide an opportunity for accountability of sorts, as members are encouraged to articulate their goals, discuss their processes, and report on what they've accomplished.

Melinda noted how she works with participants one-on-one throughout the semester, previewing and providing feedback on their human subjects applications so that when participants get to the institutional review board, "if there are any red flags, we've anticipated them and have either mitigated anything that we can do to either eliminate it or be proactive in our approach so that there aren't any huge hang-ups."

The second semester is devoted to data collection, and Melinda notes that, "you would think this would be a reprieve, but it's actually not. We actually just taught this last week, and now they're collecting data." Much of the semester is spent assisting faculty members with determining what they will do with their data once they collect it. In addition to Melinda, a faculty member from the math department, who was a member of the first cohort, voluntarily helps members of the cohort analyze and interpret statistical data.

Participants are encouraged to look outside the cohort for support as well. "One of the things we talk about is who are the people that you know on campus that you can access as resources," said Melinda. "We ask, 'Who can you utilize on campus?'" Melinda noted that it has been fun to work with cross-disciplinary teams, because, for example, somebody in the math department may help a faculty member from the English department.

Melinda noted that some faculty who have been strong in data analysis have helped other faculty "create all of the charts that will go with their presentation . . . and just to have that . . . these faculty might not have [otherwise] engaged." Sarah added, "And that's definitely the focus of the program, and I think that the thing that lots of institutions struggle with. How do you actually help faculty to collaborate with one another?" Sarah continued:

> It's a very personal relationship that the faculty members have with their students. They go into the classroom. And what happens in that classroom for the most part is really pretty much just between that faculty member and the students. [They] don't know how what [they're] doing is different than what somebody else is doing. . . . So this is part of the overall offerings that we have in trying to help faculty to realize [that they] can do something in the classroom. [They] can change things, assess the effectiveness of that and actually see the impact of it, and then hopefully replicate that. . . . This isn't a one-shot deal. But it is the only time [they are] going to participate in the SoTL program. We ask them, "How do you continue to evolve teaching and utilizing contacts with departments and across campus to actually make change happen?"

The connections that faculty make by participating in the program can help them consider ways in which they teach classes and thus help students be successful. Melinda noted:

> Good teaching is good teaching, that transcends disciplines. The lessons learned in the SoTL cohort can be applied regardless of content area. Recently, we had faculty from three different disciplines (math, biology, and physical therapy) talking about a strategy that they learned at the conference that they were each applying to their respective areas. It was so exciting for them to talk about and I think that really solidifies the transferability of teaching strategy, when you've got them cross-disciplinary.

Once participants have collected and analyzed their data, they have the following year to write up their results. At the beginning of the second year, during a fall retreat, the cohort from the previous year joins them to share the results of their SoTL inquiry, words of wisdom, and lessons learned. This has proven to be a useful process, which cohorts have described as incredibly valuable. Sarah noted that participants say that "just knowing somebody's gone through it, offers some very practical advice they can take away, and gives them kind of a bigger picture of how all the pieces of the program fit together is important."

By the end of fall semester, participants are expected to submit an abstract. "A lot of the faculty, at least the faculty that have gone through the program, haven't had to write a formal abstract," Melinda said. She noted, "Faculty don't realize that, even if they don't have their finite conclusions from their study, they can still write the abstract based on the initial analysis." The final product, then, is finished at the end of the spring semester. Participants have an opportunity to pilot their presentation or article at an in-house faculty symposium in May, with the expectation that they will seek to publish in a SoTL journal or present at a teaching and learning conference outside the college.

The cross-disciplinary connections that result from participation in the SoTL cohort at Northern Lakes Community College can do more than improve a teacher's classroom effectiveness. They can promote transformational change within the entire organization. "Don't tell anyone, but that's really what we're talking about here," said Melinda. She noted that there have been times of great contention at the college—between faculty administration, between departments, and between the college's two campuses. "Part of this is that the greater connections you can make between faculty for good helps them when things get tough," she said. "For example, when there is some kind of unrest about something going on in one department, faculty members will know someone personally to go talk to and ask about what is actually happening rather than participating in uninformed rumors and speculation."

Another benefit to the collaborative relationships built in the SoTL cohorts at Northern Lakes is that faculty can develop awareness of their role within the institution, and this can lead to improved student success. "Oftentimes people go to the things that they are not in control to change. They'll want to say 'academic advising really needs to do x, y, and z,'" said Sarah. "But having a broader picture of the organization allows faculty to understand that they can have a role in the greater student success conversation on campus. Every stakeholder has a different role at the institution, and you need to understand and focus on developing yours and not necessarily pointing fingers. And that's a culture change that takes time."

Southern Pines Technical College

Southern Pines Technical College serves around 20,000 students with approximately 500 full- and part-time faculty. The college's Teaching–Learning Center (TLC) was established in 1998, and is staffed by a director and a coordinator, both of whom are full-time faculty who receive one class release per semester plus a summer stipend to operate the TLC. The center offers several "one-off" faculty development sessions a month on a variety of topics, ranging from student advising to the school's learning management system. It offers a biennial in-house teaching and learning conference, alternating with a biennial in-house publication.

Additionally, the center facilitates FIGs, or faculty interest groups, which are teams of four to five people, both faculty and staff, whose purpose, Josh said, is to "foster collaborations between faculty from a variety of teaching disciplines and staff from across campus, to encourage data-informed decision-making about classroom practices, and to improve student success. We also include staff in these; staff have a helpful perspective a lot of the time." The guidelines for FIGs are inspired by the Professional and Organizational Development (POD) Network in Higher Education model, and are similar to but less formalized than the Cox FLC model.

The FIGs meet on a three-semester cycle, "so it would sort of be like SoTL," Josh said. "[They] investigate for a semester, then [they] implement, and then [they] publish and wrap up in the third semester." The group meets four to five times per semester, and faculty appreciate the opportunity to participate in the research. "People reiterate over and over about the FIGs, that the biggest thing it did was carve out the time and give accountability for faculty and staff to work on something together, some issue that they wanted to do but it just gets put aside because we all have a million things to do. . . . So [they're] accountable to [their] team." Faculty who participate in FIGs receive a $100 stipend.

FIGs are comprised of members who are either interested in a specific course or a theme. Recently, for example, a group of science faculty were interested in scaffolding. This group focused on the theme of scaffolding and explored how it could be applied in different courses. Faculty self-select to participate in FIGs that are of interest to them, but Josh struggled with the upcoming possibility that administration might try to mandate some FIGs. "We're not prescribing them, but coming soon we're having the guided pathways initiative and there's a lot of worry about that," Josh said. "I am going to meet with administration to see what to expect . . . are [they] going to mandate that the TLC do something? Are they going to want to try to do something [with FIGs] and maybe it doesn't go so well?"

The possibility incites strong opinions. Some of his colleagues argue that "definitely no, that sounds crazy, FIGs are a core faculty interest and it should not be prescriptive at all," Josh said. Others have advised Josh to "get ahead of it. . . . If we're going to have to do this [we] want faculty involved [with the guided pathways initiative]." Josh is concerned with the effects of administration involving itself in faculty development, and said, "I don't want to taint the FIGs brand at Eastern Shores Community College if it goes wrong," he said. "That's my fear. . . . people will say, 'Faculty are burning out. They might not want to do this [because administration] doesn't know what [they're] doing with these pathways. Why would faculty want to be involved?'"

Unlike the FIGs, the college's SoTL program is more of a solitary endeavor. Faculty can apply for support to study, as Josh noted, "what is happening in their own classrooms as opposed to outside researchers who lack sufficient knowledge of the context, discipline, or student populations researching teaching and learning to suit their [the researcher's] own purposes." Josh also said that the SoTL participants are expected to "publish their work and results in an effort to contribute to the academic field of teaching and learning in post-secondary education." Full-time instructors receive mini-sabbaticals, which release them from up to eight credit hours for a three-semester commitment; part-time instructors receive a $500 stipend upon completion of their SoTL project. Although collaborative SoTL projects are encouraged, according to TLC director Josh, thus far faculty members have opted only to do solo projects.

None of these faculty development opportunities are mandatory, yet a new policy from administration requires that faculty participate in at least five hours of faculty development per year. "People were up in arms about [the mandatory requirement], but you can count pretty much anything," said Josh. "Nothing in the TLC is required."

Despite this flexibility, professional development for faculty at Southern Pines seems to be perceived as a top-down directive, and interest in the SoTL program has waned recently because of low morale in the institution. "People feel very stressed out and over-burdened lately because there was an extra class we had to teach. It wasn't really according to our contract, but it felt like it was. . . . people just felt very burned out," said Josh. Josh also noted that SoTL is typically perceived as extra work and this has made it difficult to get faculty involved. Josh noted that he has been attempting to give SoTL a different image: "I'm trying to spin it as renewal, and that's what it should be," he said.

Josh has only been in the position of director of the TLC for a few months, and despite his own faculty status, he has encountered some resistance from other faculty members. During the first months of his position as director, he has attempted to market professional development opportunities to faculty. To do this, he surveyed faculty and had the goal to visit each department to discuss their interests and needs. Sometimes, he noted, "departments didn't want me to come . . . to their meetings. I came to the chairs meeting, which was not ideal. I sent them a marketing email and told them about our programs but haven't gotten the results from all that yet."

Despite a seeming resistance to the offerings of the TLC, Josh has noticed that the activities faculty participate in do produce a "ripple effect of collaboration." He cites the SoTL program as an example that has encouraged collaboration because it allowed faculty members to become experts on a topic. For example, one faculty member did a study on plagiarism, and after completing the study he is now perceived as an expert on campus. Consequently, this faculty member has also made many presentations to colleagues on the topic, and was consulted by administration and asked to play a part in writing their academic integrity policy. "It keeps snowballing and rolling afterward," Josh noted as he recalled successful initiatives. For example, he noted how another faculty member had started out in a FIG on student motivation, and was inspired to extend that research to do a SoTL project on intrinsic and extrinsic motivation and increasing motivation in online courses.

Josh has also observed the beneficial effect of people making bridges across disciplines, including opportunities for transfer and technical faculty to connect. "People need to know what happens in other departments," he said. "If we know what other people are doing we can talk more intelligently about it, and then also be involved in it; hopefully we can shape where it's going." Josh believed that even the "one-off" sessions that the TLC offers can foster collegiality through stress relief and social connection. "That's a big part of what we do," he said. "We don't want to force people to do it but there's a lot of people who, I think, would benefit from the sessions who might not jump out at it but who almost need it."

Eastern Shores Community College

Eastern Shores Community College, a two-campus community college in the Northeast, was founded in 1987 and has an enrollment of approximately 12,000 students and approximately 400 full- and part-time faculty members. Like Northern Lakes and Southern Pines, Eastern Shores offers transfer programs as well as technical and career training programs. Eastern Shores was an early adopter of the SoTL, dating back to the early 1990s, because a faculty member participated as a faculty fellow in the Carnegie Academy for the Scholarship of Teaching and Learning (CASTL) and brought the principles back to the institution. Thus, the concept of SoTL has been infused into the culture of the institution almost since its inception, and both faculty and staff participate in the SoTL activities.

"People don't even know what it stands for, but they'll be like, 'Are you going to SoTL?'" said Nancy, faculty member and co-coordinator of the SoTL program at Eastern Shores. She added, "The president and provost use it a lot too." Eastern Shores does not have a centralized center for faculty development, but the provost asked Nancy and another faculty member to lead faculty development, which, Nancy noted, "was still a work in progress".

Professional development at Eastern Shores falls under a broad umbrella within the college, and Nancy said that "with the regular professional development model, not a lot of people were coming to workshops because of them being mostly one-shot workshops." Nancy and her colleague, co-coordinators of the SoTL program, receive one course release per semester to administer it, but, as Nancy noted, "the problem is that even though [we get] two course reassign times a year, which is a lot, it's still not enough to do everything, and still do a good job with teaching."

Nancy described the meaning of SoTL at Eastern Shores by claiming that Eastern Shores "had the classic understanding [of SoTL]. We learned about this notion of conducting action research and sharing it . . .. and the dissemination piece was the trickiest because a lot of community college faculty are teaching five courses, so they want to try it out but then to actually publish wasn't easy." Despite this classic understanding, SoTL has evolved at the college to move away from action research and instead toward faculty taking on broader projects within a loose configuration of faculty learning communities. "We don't follow [Cox's model] exactly," Nancy said. "But we use elements of it."

Last year, Nancy and her colleague launched an initiative to study student retention and course completion. The aim was for instructors to have a goal of 100% course completion. The initiative was called "Creating a Culture of Persistence and Student Success," and the goal of the initiative was to increase the persistence rate from fall to spring by 50%. The initiative is faculty led, but administrators are also active in the project. For example, the dean of enrollment attended some of the group's meetings in order to provide them with relevant data about enrollment. The provost at Eastern Shores also asked the group to put together eighteen SoTL-related sessions; these sessions included staff from all areas of the college, including faculty, financial aid personnel, administrative assistants, and institutional research personnel.

In the first year of the initiative, twenty faculty members from sixteen disciplines committed to identify one course in which they would try to retain 100% of the students. They created a blog where everyone logged what the number of students on their roster on the first day of class and checked in with each other throughout the semester to see how they were doing with retaining students. This allowed them to share strategies around retention. At the end of the semester, they calculated the results from the initiative and distributed a survey to faculty, asking them what strategies to bolster retention were most effective.

The first year did not show significant improvement (most retained the same amount of students or retention only increased a bit); however, faculty noticed an unintended consequence of the initiative. "What we found out," said Nancy, "was that it was a collaborative effort. So the discussion around the water cooler was not complaints, but about student persistence and success. The conversation was much more productive." The cohort of faculty who participated in the persistence project met monthly to talk about their experiences. Depending on the time in the semester, attendance ranged from twelve to twenty-four faculty members, along with a few administrators. Participation in the initiative was voluntary, though faculty did receive $350. About this, Nancy commented that it was "kind of a drop in the bucket for the work they're doing, but at least it's an honorarium."

The initiative is now in its second year and the cohort has increased to thirty-three faculty members from sixteen different disciplines. This time, the initiative included adjunct faculty and broadened its scope to collaborate with financial aid, student accounts, and advising enrollment. Nancy attributes the increase in faculty participation to an information session that was offered about the 100% completion initiative at Eastern Shore's annual half-day winter retreat. "Everyone who came to the retreat—we pretty much strong-armed them," she said, laughing. "We went around with a clipboard and told some of the faculty, had they not been there, they may not have joined."

Despite these "strong-arm tactics," Nancy still considers the motivation for participation in the initiative to be primarily from a faculty-led professional learning culture. Faculty members' enthusiasm was also a big part of its success. Nancy noted, "We had so many of the returning faculty and they got up and talked about their experience. One person had won the League for Innovation Award last year and he listed among his accomplishments at [Eastern Shores] being part of the 100% group," she said. "I think people are enjoying being part of it. . . . I think the part-time faculty are looking to be part of the community."

Nancy believes that voluntary participation in initiatives like the 100% group are essential for SoTL to be effective. Recently, she was asked to lead a mandatory new faculty orientation, and she noticed "a stark difference between when it's voluntary and when it's mandatory." Faculty complained that the mandatory meeting was too much work and that it did not suit their teaching style. They also noted that it took too much time. Faculty attitudes at the cohort meetings were negative and uncooperative. Although a survey at the end indicated that most participants found the experience worthwhile, the difference in morale and enthusiasm between a voluntary and mandatory workshop was notable. "When it's voluntary, there is excitement built in and they want to do it," said Nancy.

A lack of confidence in senior leadership at the college has caused faculty morale to drop in general, but Nancy believes that morale within the SoTL group is higher than average because faculty spend time talking about what they care about. "People do research on topics relevant to what we do in the classroom and then share out," she said. "I think they feel they're being heard." She noted the particular kind of passion for students and teaching that she observes in her faculty colleagues:

> Most of us view community college education through a social justice lens and we feel that the idea of non-completion means that we're taking the student's money. We believe in equity and social justice, so trying to find ways for students to succeed and achieve, hopefully either through obtaining a career or earning a bachelor's . . . we've even had a couple of people in our group who have helped students get all the way to medical school. It's a very committed group of faculty, so that's what we care about. We care about student success.

Nancy feels that this passion positions community college faculty to contribute to SoTL scholarship. "For community colleges, because we don't have discipline-specific research, this is where SoTL should live," she said. "I think we should be looking at the community college as very key to implementing SoTL, but a completely different animal than a four-year institution. We are completely teaching-centered."

Nancy emphasized how the needs of community college students are different than those in more elite institutions. She characterized elite institutions as "places that have very few students that actually need extra support, so [the faculty there] are trying to work with a very small percentage of their students. They're trying to up the percentages," she said. "But, in the community college, the students who may need extra support are who we have. We have a complete over-representation of students of color, first gen[eration] students, and low-income students. SoTL is all about thinking about how to serve these students. We need to do research within our classroom and if we can do more broad-based SoTL inquiries, that's the only way we can find out what's going on with these students."

Unfortunately, because community college faculty teach such heavy loads, it is difficult for them to find the time to conduct SoTL research effectively. Nancy and her colleague are working on a proposal that would enable faculty to apply for one course reassignment to study persistence and retention efforts in their classrooms. "The only way we could do it is if [we] could save enough students that it would break even or [we] would save a little money or something," Nancy said. "But if you're teaching five courses per semester, I mean [teachers] can barely keep [their] heads above water."

Nancy maintained that SoTL should be faculty-led. She said, "I know a lot of colleges have administrators that run SoTL. But they would benefit from partnering with a co-director that was a faculty member . . . because I think the perception is that if SoTL comes from an administrator, it feels top-down. Everybody has the same goals, but still, with another faculty member, you know they're understanding that you're going through the same thing."

IN CONVERSATION ABOUT
THE BENEFITS OF THE SoTL

After completing individual interviews with faculty developers from Northern Lakes Community College, Southern Pines Technical College, and Eastern Shores Community College, the faculty developers from each of the institutions reconvened for a virtual conversation about SoTL, FLCs, and faculty development. Participants noted that each of their respective institutions had slightly different interpretations of SoTL, but that all were firmly committed to the active research component.

Nancy began the discussion about the definition of the SoTL by sharing with the others the purpose of SoTL at Eastern Shores: "Eastern Shores has a loose definition of SoTL. For us, SoTL has been a vehicle to bring the faculty together around issues that we care about." Since Eastern Shores has been engaged with SoTL the longest of the three respective institutions, it felt appropriate that Nancy was forthright in sharing her experiences. She also touched on the benefits to faculty members by situating the SoTL as collaborative. "SoTL provides a way for faculty from all different disciplines to work together. We have a very loose structure in that we have monthly meetings, a book club, a launch group, and a 100% course completion group," Nancy explained.

Josh, from Southern Pines Technical College, agreed with Nancy that an institution must make SoTL their own. Josh said, "SoTL has infused some enthusiasm among faculty whose morale is a little low because things are somewhat unsettled in our college right now. SoTL gives us an opportunity to talk in a positive manner about change as opposed to complaining about things we can't get done. Instead of coming from the top down, faculty have been really involved in planning SoTL initiatives."

Northern Lakes Community College is the newest to SoTL practices, and Melinda noted that how SoTL is implemented is "structured" at Northern Lakes. She also made it a point to say that there was still a select group of people participating, but "the initiatives are expanding and word is getting out, which is super exciting." Though she was excited about what was happening at Northern Lakes, she also said, "I strive for the multiple opportunities and access points into SoTL."

The SoTL program at Northern Lakes follows the tenets of SoTL the most formally of the three institutions, and Melinda was interested to discover that others interpreted it more loosely than her institution did. This seemed to present her with future possibilities and she exclaimed that she learned that "SOTL doesn't necessarily have to just be a scholarly research study that is going through the IRB. Instead, there can be other ways to tap into that tangential work that surrounds it, that it's really rooted in, and so foundational to what I think SoTL really is."

All three faculty developers agreed that SoTL work has the potential to be contagious. Faculty share their experiences with SoTL and get excited about participating. Josh pointed to reasons that he thought faculty got excited by saying, "I think it's because they get to talk about their teaching, and there aren't a lot of opportunities to do that. It's easy to be siloed, and even within a department, it's easy to be on our own and to not have those conversations."

A question was posed to the participants: Why does it matter that departments and disciplines are siloed? Melinda responded quickly to this question by noting that "good teaching transcends content area." She added, "We can learn about good teaching and how we can apply that in our particular subject area across disciplines, and so there is value in that. It's easy to be in our office or in our class-room. In doing that, our scope gets narrower and narrower in how we interact and engage with our students and create curriculum. [The connections made in SoTL activities] are a way to have good conversations with people who are excited about this too."

Nancy, from Eastern Shores, commented on the diversity that exists within the community college: "It's almost like several institutions in one." Nancy, for example, teaches developmental English and was working with a colleague who taught Physics II. Though they had very different student populations with very different expectations, they realized there was value in sharing strategies that they could both use. In their 100% course completion cohort, the physics teacher suggested that they email every student who did not attend the first day of class for the semester. Nancy said, "Okay, that seems like a very easy strategy, but I had been teaching for twenty-five years and had never done that before."

Despite the vast differences between their disciplines and their students, these two faculty members were able to share teaching strategies that benefited them both. Hearing the struggles that each individual department had with their students "sort of demystifies things," Nancy said, and paints a broader picture of the student experience for faculty to contextualize their students' situations. The opportunity to hear from other faculty and find out everyone's concerns assists all in working toward a common cause. Josh noted that the collaborative environment "sort of eliminates the pettiness that sometimes happens when departments [think] their own department is more important or whatever."

Building trust is essential for SoTL activities to be successful. Faculty need to feel confident that if they reveal their struggles and questions, they will not face repercussions or embarrassment. Nancy said, "We always say, 'What happens in SoTL stays in SoTL.'" Melinda observed that trust-building occurs in SoTL cohorts. "It becomes a pretty tight group," she said. "It's an amazing difference between fall and spring when they've traveled together and worked together. . . . I notice that there's a guard up in the fall but there definitely isn't that guard up in the spring."

The benefits of this collegiality can extend to the students as well. Nancy, Josh, and Melinda agreed that students are also able to witness the collegiality among faculty, which can cause students to be more confident and enthusiastic about their situation in the college. It is also valuable for students to observe their teachers participating in research and continuing their own learning. "Psychologically it's much better for all of us," said Josh.

Without exception, lack of time and resources were cited as the greatest barriers to community college faculty's ability to conduct SoTL research. The need to keep faculty participation voluntary was also mentioned repeatedly. The challenge for all was finding a balance that could allow faculty members the time and compensation to conduct SoTL research. Unlike their four-year university counterparts, research is not built into the reward system for community college faculty. Yet, because of the nature of their jobs and of their students, community college faculty have vast experience and knowledge that, if shared, has the potential to benefit teachers at all institutions of higher education.

EXPLORING SoTL'S ROLE
IN THE COMMUNITY COLLEGE

Melinda, Josh, and Nancy were keenly aware of the role that community colleges play for underserved students. "We have the lowest tuition in our state," said Melinda from Northern Lakes, adding that "making higher education affordable" has been a big focus of their institution for the last twenty years. One of the institution's strategic goals is academic excellence, and striving to meet that goal was the impetus that led to Northern Lakes's engagement with SoTL practices, Melinda noted: "We felt we should be modeling [academic excellence], and we should have this reflective lens and be looking at ourselves as practitioners."

Sarah, the co-facilitator of SoTL at Northern Lakes, added that all too often, the lens from which to examine programs is an external one, and most research on community colleges tends to be done by universities. Sarah said that there is "nothing preventing us from actually looking at what we do within the community college and actually learning from that from a pedagogical perspective." Melinda argued that the fact that Northern Lakes is working with community college students and the closeness to this reality of day-to-day work in the community college makes SoTL research relevant:

> I mean, I don't know . . . that sounds arrogant on my part but . . . if we're in the classroom and have heavy teaching loads and we can be making a difference with a population that is not necessarily your highfliers from high school or in higher education, where all these different strategies, design, components, and feedback, can really make a difference . . . [then] we need to be doing this research and sharing it and disseminating it among us.

Nancy made a similar point. During the conversation, Nancy described how she is currently enrolled in a doctoral program for faculty in higher education and many of her classmates are from more prestigious schools in the Northeast. The curriculum of her doctoral program has a social justice and equity lens through which the entire program is administered, and she noted that the other people in her cohort have very few students that belong to the marginalized groups that face the problems that social justice and equity educational programs seek to address.

In fact, many of these schools are attempting to increase the percentages of marginalized students in their enrollment. "But," she said, "that's who we have!" Nancy argued that community college faculty need to do the research within their classrooms, and if they can do more broad-based studies, they can contribute to the scholarship of how to teach all students most effectively.

HOW DOES THE IMPLEMENTATION
OF SoTL AFFECT CAMPUS CULTURE?

A dominant theme that emerged in the conversations with Nancy, Melinda, Sarah, and Josh was the effect of SoTL activities on collaboration, and the effect of that collaboration on campus culture. It was clear that the three institutions had similarities and these were shared across all community colleges. But there were distinct differences among them, too. The greatest commonality among all three colleges was that all participants from the three institutions, Northern Lakes, Southern Pines, and Eastern Shores, agreed that a collaborative community college culture made for a better culture. In some cases, this meant collaboration between faculty and administration. In other cases, it meant collaboration among faculty and across disciplines. Some experienced both of these phenomena.

Northern Lakes Community College reported a high level of collaboration both among faculty and between faculty and administration. This was likely exemplified by the fact that both a faculty member and administrator, Melinda and Sarah, chose to take part in the interview to explain their mutual roles in introducing the SoTL program at their institution. Early in our conversation, Melinda noted that "the faculty, administration, and the union get along. I know in some community colleges, if they are a union state, it can be contentious sometimes, but it isn't that way at Northern Lakes." Indeed, two of the community colleges featured in this chapter, Northern Lakes Community College and Eastern Shores Community College, had faculty unions, and, in contrast to Northern Lakes, the relationship between the faculty union and administration at Eastern Shores appeared to be contentious.

"We're in a difficult situation right now because we just had a vote of no confidence with our president," said Nancy from Eastern Shores. Nancy proffered this toward the end of our conversation, with a note of embarrassment. She added, "But our faculty are very committed and I think the vote was meant . . . that this was the only way to make some changes." This revelation was surprising to all in the conversation, because, prior to this, Nancy had spoken so positively about the combined efforts of faculty, administration, and staff with their retention initiative. At the same time, Nancy was the most adamant of the participants about the importance of SoTL initiatives being faculty-led, and the danger of top-down directives.

Sarah, the administrator from Northern Lakes, shared her perspective, but seemed to have a more pragmatic view. "I think we've done fairly well," she said. "We had a new president that came in about seven years ago and he has really worked hard at [the faculty–administration relationship]. I think there was a little bit more friction between faculty and administration with the prior president. [The current president's] focus is really on focusing our strengths and developing our strengths and not necessarily succumbing to the bitterness that sometimes the institution [can experience]."

Southern Pines Technical College does not have a faculty union, and statewide, community college faculty are not allowed to use the title of "professor." "It's not a union state and it's not a union culture," Josh said. "We do have a faculty association . . . but the faculty association doesn't seem to have a lot of power." He noted that the state in which Southern Pines is located is an "at-will" state, and that statewide regulations apply to all community colleges. "I don't know how much you know about [our state]," he said. "But we're all instructors [in the community colleges], we're not professors." The ambiguousness of the system seemed to be a source of unease for the faculty there: "[We're] on a nine-month contract, and everybody says it's hard to get fired, but [we] get this letter every year that says

'Oh, yeah, you're getting a job next year. Congratulations.'" Josh shared this laughingly but with an undertone of some resentment.

In fact, the differences among the campus cultures at the three institutions seemed to be directly tied to the faculty relationship with administration. Northern Lakes reported the highest level of mutual collaboration and, though their introduction of SoTL was recent, seemed to have the highest level of faculty engagement. Rather than having to recruit participants, they consistently had more people interested than were able to participate.

Eastern Shores reported strong relationships among faculty, but an adversarial relationship with administration. While their SoTL program was robust and faculty seemed particularly energized about the retention project, there were suggestions of having to "strong arm" faculty into participating. The faculty at Eastern Shores, where the faculty–administration divide seemed particularly wide, were repeatedly described by Nancy as burned out, overburdened, and resistant to participating in SoTL activities.

All agreed that collaboration improves culture. Each participant offered many reasons for improved collaboration on their campuses. Involving faculty in the broader needs of the institution seemed to increase their engagement and even affected the choices they made in the classroom. "How fantastic is it that instead of complaining about low enrollments and decreased budgets, that faculty are actually doing things that they have control over?" Josh said. "It's much more . . . psychologically it's much better for all of us," agreed Melinda. Achieving a balance between empowerment and autonomy, while still providing direction and resources, would seem to be the most effective way to promote cross-disciplinary, cross-campus collaboration as well as increase faculty morale.

WHAT EFFECT DOES SoTL HAVE ON TEACHING?

Increased collaboration improves campus culture and the situation of both faculty, administrators, and other staff members. While it may be relatively simple to determine the impact of SoTL on faculty through surveys and interviews, understanding the actual effect on students and teaching proves more difficult. Because individual SoTL studies vary widely from teacher to teacher and from discipline to discipline, it is difficult to quantify the overall impact within any single institution.

Yet, studies show (regardless of the level of rigor of each study) that faculty change their pedagogy as a result of SoTL and completing an SoTL project (Burns, 2017). "It opens up a culture of trying new things and being open to trying new things" said Josh. Nancy observed that participating in SoTL research "increases reflection and motivation" in teachers. However, SoTL research does not take place in isolation. One of the most integral tenets of the SoTL is the requirement to share the results of one's scholarly teaching and research. When it takes place in an open, collaborative, sharing environment (as opposed to a competitive environment), this sharing almost certainly impacts teaching.

FACULTY-LED VERSUS TOP-DOWN FACULTY DEVELOPMENT

Throughout the interviews and focus groups, the theme of faculty-led versus top-down faculty development emerged again and again from faculty developers. It arose often enough to warrant its own discussion. Faculty and administrators alike maintain that the best faculty development is faculty-led. Faculty-led faculty development is the most effective way to engage faculty participation, enthusiasm, and collaboration. Top-down initiatives for professional development tend to result in resistance and cynicism.

Yet, despite this universal agreement, faculty development initiatives, including coordinated SoTL initiatives, often continue to be perceived as top-down mandates rather than organic, faculty-led programs designed to meet faculty needs as well as improve performance. To look for ways to foster such collaboration through faculty-led development, we now turn to collaboration theory

(Thomson & Perry, 2006; Wood & Gray, 1991;) to explore the ways in which organizations can foster a collaborative culture.

In addition to an exploration of themes that emerged from the data itself, this book seeks to understand how the data about faculty development in community colleges resonates with collaboration theory. As noted above, collaboration is a process that occurs over time (Thomson & Perry, 2006). It is a nonlinear process that manifests in "personal relationships, psychological contracts, and informal understandings and commitments" (Thomson & Perry, 2006, p. 22). The integrative elements of collaboration theory need to supersede the more formal organizational roles, and finding a balance between these elements may promote long-lasting collaboration.

ASPECTS OF COLLABORATION
WITHIN FACULTY DEVELOPMENT

The collaboration process can be understood as having five nonsequential dimensions: governance, administration, autonomy, mutuality, and norms of trust and reciprocity. Those wishing to foster collaboration should seek a balance among all five dimensions. Exploration of how the examples of collaboration in each of the cases featured in this chapter fit into the five dimensions of collaboration can help illuminate the ways in which collaboration can be fostered in institutions of higher education.

Governance

The governance dimension of collaboration requires that partners determine the rules that govern the process jointly; the power must be shared. This can be difficult in a higher education institution where power is often organized hierarchically, and where administrators appear to or actually do have more power within the organization than faculty. In fact, for the governance dimension to function effectively, all participants must be aware that they are all equally responsible for reaching agreement. That is, if they have shared interests in reaching a shared desired outcome, there must be an openness to sharing information and mutually respecting opinions.

Allowing for consensus to emerge requires time and an understanding that total agreement will unlikely be reached on everything, but that respect for all parties will allow for all parties to support a decision once it is made. Working collectively to formulate rules for joint decision-making is challenging, and perhaps the burden for collective governance in collaboration falls more heavily on administration.

In all three cases featured in this chapter, it is clear that administration is assumed to have a disproportionate degree of authority in the organization. As discussed above, Northern Lakes Community College seemed to have the least hierarchical relationship between administration and faculty and the highest level of faculty engagement in SoTL opportunities offered. The program administered at Northern Lakes had been jointly created by an administrator and a faculty member (Melinda and Sarah), yet the administrator voluntarily stayed out of the way and let the faculty member administer the program with faculty, forgoing getting any sort of credit or recognition for the program.

Eastern Shores Community College clearly had tension between faculty and administration, yet the faculty was able to exert its power enough to create a kind of us-against-them situation in which faculty came together in spite of the administration. In Southern Pines Technical College, where faculty perceived themselves to have the least power, participation in SoTL opportunities offered was least appreciated. For collaboration to be successful, governance, or who is in charge of making the rules, should be determined jointly.

Administration

Another key dimension of collaboration that seems to be difficult for community colleges to agree on is the administration, or administering, dimension. Administration is the nuts and bolts of implementation. Collaborations must have some sort of organization in order to accomplish their purpose, and this is where the traditional top-down hierarchical structure can get in the way of collaboration.

The typical top-down structure of people at the top making the rules and then instructing someone to enforce them may be what most consider when discussing administration. These administrative roles are important, and perhaps even essential, for accomplishing certain aspects of operating a college. But for collaboration to thrive, hierarchical relationships must become more horizontal. Faculty are decentralized by nature—each have their own disciplines and classrooms—therefore, they are focused on their own subjects and often lack the time and resources to develop a complete picture of the organization.

For the administrator to foster collaboration, it is essential to honor and understand this decentralization and to respect the perspectives that each person brings, as Sarah, from Northern Lakes, demonstrates when she says, "I think it is the partnership between administration and faculty. I try to give Melinda the stage because I think it's received much better when it comes from full-time faculty." At the same time, it is important for faculty to recognize their sometimes more limited perspective and allow an interdependency to develop. According to Thomson and Perry (2006), the different partners involved in a collaboration include "convener, advocate, technical assistance provider, facilitator, and funder, each of which is necessary for the collaboration as a whole to achieve its goals" (p. 26). Vulnerability is required on both sides to allow the necessary roles to evolve.

Autonomy

The autonomy dimension of collaboration theory might help explain the disconnect that can occur in the community college setting when different collaboration partners' self-interests are overlooked in the governance or the administration dimensions. Naturally, in any relationship, or in any organization, there is a distinction between self-interest and collective interest. The individual feels a need to defend their individuality and well-being. At the same time, being part of an organization or relationship suggests that the individual desires to contribute to the collective interest, or at least understands it.

This conflict can be destructive and frustrating, but it can also bring a dynamic tension that can enliven the collaborative process and help to explain the unexpected, synergistic outcomes that can occur in the black box of collaboration. When the organization's collaboration goals conflict with the individual's goals, the individual's sense of identity can be lost, which can stall or stymie the collaboration process.

The faculty at Eastern Shores illustrate this tension in their project for student retention. Their endeavor was faculty-driven, and at first they did not perceive the need for administrative involvement. Nancy said, "We designed what we wanted to try, but then we had our enrollment team come in and explain things. We didn't even know the difference among all the terms. We asked things like, 'What's the difference between persistence and retention?' We did research on that and then [the dean of enrollment] came and explained and brought in all kinds of data. So then we had [the Institutional Research Board] run a bunch of numbers trying to figure out what population is not persisting."

The project began with the faculty group working toward their goals individually, without seeking support or involvement from administrative entities within the institution. As they became more involved with the project, they began to understand how other groups previously perceived as separate and not relevant to their purposes, could, in fact, assist them in their endeavor. The original tension experienced was overcome by the discovery of a collective interest. Working to find commonalities in differences can bring transformational results, and perhaps help bring balance to the dimensions of collaboration.

Mutuality

In considering the balance of the five dimensions in the cases discussed in this chapter, the mutuality dimension can weigh the heaviest. This is the area where faculty, no matter how they came to participate in a collaborative process, whether top-down mandate or faculty-led, perceive the most benefit.

As Nancy pointed out in her discussion of the mandatory new faculty orientation program, the ending survey indicated that "everybody thought it was worthwhile." She knew, though, that many resisted this orientation. Although new faculty initially resisted attending the orientation, likely because of a perceived lack of autonomy, in the end, the experience was perceived as beneficial. For collaboration to succeed, collaborating partners must find some sort of benefit in the sharing of information.

It is essential for the relationships in a collaborative partnership to be interdependent despite the differing interests of individuals. Somehow, administrators must learn how to allow autonomy; at the same time, when faculty are willing to give up something in their own interest to benefit the commonality, both sides can benefit. If both parties share the common goal of serving students, then finding ways to reach that common goal is mutually beneficial to all parties—teachers, administrators, and most importantly, students.

Norms of Reciprocity and Trust

Building these mutually beneficial collaborations requires reciprocity and trust. Like the other dimensions of collaboration theory, building this type of social capital requires time. At its most basic level, reciprocity involves a kind of "I will if you will" mentality; it is the need for both partners to believe that both sides are giving and sharing information. Trust takes it a step further, and assumes that all partners act in good faith, with honesty and integrity. Building these norms cannot be forced but requires the time and emotional investment needed to build personal relationships.

As observed in the discussion with Josh from Southern Pines and Nancy from Eastern Shores, faculty had developed an "us-against-them" mentality with the administration. At Eastern Shores, the environment seemed to foster collegiality and trust among faculty, but not across the institution. This reciprocity and trust may be what motivated them to pursue the 100% completion project despite a lack of trust in administration because they had banded together in pursuit of a goal.

There seemed to be less trust among faculty, as well as between faculty and administration, at Southern Pines; perhaps the insecurity faculty felt about their jobs contributed to this and prevented them from feeling empowered to initiate change. Because faculty at Southern Pines are not guaranteed a returning contract each year, faculty there may feel a sense of uncertainty and a need to protect their own self-interest (the need to keep their job). In addition to inhibiting the development of the norms of reciprocity and trust, the need for self-protection interferes and causes imbalance with the mutuality and autonomy dimensions because individuals are less inclined to work toward the good of the organization, but rather toward protecting their own interests.

LOOKING AHEAD

The themes that emerged from conversations with Melinda, Sarah, Josh, and Nancy can be understood through the dimensions of collaboration theory, and understanding how these dimensions fit into the framework of collaboration and faculty development more broadly can prompt understanding of faculty development at both the individual and institutional levels. Understanding the elements that affect collaboration can assist community college faculty and administrators in creating an environment that promotes improved collegiality and potentially enhanced opportunities for more effective teaching.

The following chapter, chapter 4, features faculty developers' work in a time of uncertainty and explores how faculty developers shifted faculty development in response to the COVID-19 pandemic. The faculty developers featured in the following chapter seek to continue faculty development but also direct their gaze to the ways in which they must pivot during this new era.

Chapter Four

Case Studies of Faculty Developers and Faculty at Community Colleges

Responding to an Era of Uncertainty

Education at U.S. community colleges had been in transition before the start of the COVID-19 pandemic in 2020. U.S. community colleges, sensitive to their role in providing open access to a wide variety of students, have long grappled with both their relevance and their service to a wide demographic of students. Faculty developers at community colleges, such as the developers featured in the previous chapter, had been committed to faculty needs before the pandemic era, and their role as often the sole faculty development person at their institution had already encompassed many different aspects of working with faculty.

Yet, when higher education faced the disruption of the pandemic in March 2020, how did faculty developers respond? This chapter seeks to illuminate how particular individuals reached out to faculty at their institutions in an effort to transition course teaching to the online space. As the pandemic continued, faculty developers had to continue to support faculty during a time of uncertainty. Many traditional campuses continued, over summer and fall 2020, to reevaluate what the community college experience was for students if it no longer included the on-campus experience that it did before the pandemic.

As programs and courses moved to online delivery models in mid-spring 2020, the community college experience, as a whole, became increasingly decentralized. Already quite decentralized due to the nature of housing a wide variety of programs, community colleges sought to utilize faculty developers in a way that united efforts across programs. Though online teaching was a course delivery mode used before the pandemic era, the sheer number of faculty who learned to deliver courses in hybrid, online, or HyFlex formats grew exponentially. As a result, courses taught from online platforms propelled higher education fully into the e-learning space and community colleges were pressed to undergo the "stress test" of COVID-19. Currently, it is unknown how many institutions— community colleges and four-year institutions alike—will make it through the current challenges.

This book makes reference to the "first full pandemic year of 2020–2021," as this is how the COVID-19 era has been referenced in the *Chronicle of Higher Education* (Alexander, 2020). As in chapter 3, this chapter features institutions and their respective faculty developers' work with faculty; yet, in this chapter, faculty developers' responses to planning for faculty development for the first full pandemic year are featured. The data collected from these participants and institutions reflects how faculty development was forced to pivot due to the pandemic; in many ways, this meant that faculty development moved away from traditional practices, such as the SoTL and FLCs, and toward new, just-in-time (JiT) initiatives.

Changes featured throughout this chapter include the ways that faculty developers urged collaboration with faculty around environmental and instructional changes, as well as around significant alterations to the student experience. As a whole, this chapter questions what features of faculty development might be sustained beyond the pandemic era.

INSTITUTIONS AND PARTICIPANTS

Table 4.1.   **Responses to the COVID-19 Pandemic: Cases of Faculty Developers at Community Colleges**

Community College	Region of United States	Size of Institution and Distinguishing Features
Southeast Valley Community College	Southeast	18,000 students, five campuses; faculty are not unionized
Desert Plains Community College	Southwest	220,000 students, ten campuses; faculty are (as of February 2019) not unionized
River Junction Community College	Midwest	14,000 students, one campus, two satellite campuses; faculty are unionized

This chapter, which presents data collected during the COVID-19 pandemic, features three distinct contexts: Southeast Valley Community College in the U.S. Southeast; Desert Plains Community College in the U.S. Southwest; and River Junction Community College in the U.S. Midwest (all names of people and places are pseudonyms). The cases of Southeast Valley and Desert Plains are depicted from faculty developers' perspectives. The case of River Junction Community College is depicted from a faculty perspective, using the results of a survey that was distributed to faculty during the pandemic; this survey was created to highlight the needs of faculty during the pandemic era.

Data collected from Southeast Valley Community College included an interview with Michael Jacobs, a faculty developer. Michael has been in his faculty development director position for about thirteen years and also holds a faculty position at Southeast Valley. Michael's journey as a faculty developer emerged from a part-time role at his institution, and it was in a role of teaching students in the cosmetology program at Southeast Valley that Michael learned to be innovative and craft lessons focused on teaching.

Because the cosmetology program at Southeast Valley required that students hold a license to teach, the methods of teaching class that Michael designed more than fifteen years ago became a primer for his current faculty development position. Michael's relationship with the vice provost for academic affairs also helped him make his acumen for faculty development a reality at Southeast Valley. This administrator also helped Michael become the faculty member who created and delivered faculty development for multiple units at the community college. Since then, Michael has worked with new, full-time faculty at Southeast Valley and has also started a faculty development program for adjuncts. In addition to working for his own institution, Michael works with other institutions to deliver faculty professional development.

The second faculty developer featured in this chapter, Annette Hansen, is the Center for Teaching and Learning (CTL) director at one of the ten Desert Plains Community College branches. Desert Plains, as a system, is unique because it has prioritized faculty development, and the system includes a main Center for Teaching and Learning that focuses on district-wide programming as well as smaller CTLs at each of the ten campuses. Though each of the ten branches has its own CTL, Annette noted that they differ in their priorities and the work they do with faculty.

CTL director positions at the two largest branches are permanent positions and are also faculty positions, whereas at about half of the branches, CTL directors are management positions (not faculty positions). Finally, a few of the campus branches rotate the faculty development director role between faculty members. Annette noted that having a faculty position at the CTL at one of Desert Plains' largest campus branches has allowed her to be respected by faculty. She said that "faculty respect faculty," and cited the ability to fully relate to teaching practices as one of the central reasons that a respectful relationship can be actualized between faculty and CTL directors who are also faculty.

The third institution featured in this chapter is River Junction Community College. Data collected from this institution consisted of the results of a survey that was sent to faculty about their experiences with faculty development during the pandemic era. Located in an affluent suburb in the Midwest, River Junction Community College serves approximately 14,000 students, with 318 full-time faculty members and 538 adjunct faculty members. Traditionally, faculty development at River Junction fell under the domain of staff and organizational development within the college, but recently, the institution created a specific department devoted to faculty development with two full-time staff members (a director and a coordinator).

The full-time faculty at River Junction is unionized; as a stipulation of their contract, they are required to participate in Professional Development Days (PDD), a week-long, in-house conference at the beginning of each semester. PDD consists of various sessions offered on teaching and learning, educational technology, student engagement, and employee engagement. Adjunct faculty members are typically required to attend one evening department meeting per semester, which they are paid to attend. In addition to this, adjunct faculty members are encouraged, but not required, to participate in the campus-wide PDD. Additionally, the college offers a voluntary Adjunct Certification Program, which is a series of classes offered outside of traditional working hours focused on teaching and learning; upon completion of this program, adjunct faculty are awarded a stipend.

DATA COLLECTION AND ANALYSIS

Like data featured in chapter 3, the semi-structured interviews with the two faculty developers, Michael Jacobs and Annette Hansen, were transcribed and coded. Yet, the aim for the interviews with these faculty developers focused on the pandemic era and the challenges that this era presented. The questions that guided the interviews are featured in Appendix B. Interviews were conducted and recorded using Zoom, an online communication platform.

Data from interviews with the two faculty developers was analyzed through establishing inductive and deductive codes, with deductive coding constructs coming from recently published articles that attended to COVID-19's effect on the educational landscape. Such codes included environmental and instructional change as well as significant alterations to the student experience. Attention to institutions' increased effort to reach students who come from disadvantaged or underserved populations was also prioritized.

To provide faculty development that responded to these challenges, both Michael and Annette focused on presenting faculty with some baseline guidance about how to move courses online. To reach a wide audience of faculty, Michael and Annette had to assess the bigger picture of what faculty needed on their campuses. Often, that included new training on online tools and learning management platforms.

The data from River Junction Community College were collected from a survey administered to the entire faculty during spring 2021. This survey's intent was to explore the faculty perspective of the impact and lessons learned during the transition to online teaching during the COVID-19 shutdown. The 10-question survey had a response rate of 22% (176 responses out of 785 full- and part-time faculty members). The combination of Likert scale and open-ended questions (see the full survey in Appendix C) on the survey included the following:

1. What were the most challenging aspects of the transition to entirely online teaching and learning?
2. How satisfied are you with the college's performance in regard to meeting the ever-changing needs of faculty brought about as a result of the pandemic?
3. Describe how you had to change your expectations.
4. Did you have to change your course materials?
5. Which of the following best describes how your role as a faculty member changed as a result of the pandemic?
6. How significantly was your mental health affected by the experience of transitioning to all online courses and work during the pandemic?

7. Where do you go to find the resources you need to support your teaching?
8. What new collaborations have you seen at the college as a result of COVID-19?
9. What changes have you made in your teaching that will continue once we are "back to normal?"
10. Additional Comments:

The answers from the survey were tabulated and the open-ended comments were transcribed and coded. Like the semi-structured interviews with faculty developers featured at the beginning of this chapter, the questions on the survey were designed to elicit perspectives on the pandemic era and the challenges that this era presented to faculty development. The survey was sent electronically to faculty via the college's Office of Institutional Research.

The survey data was analyzed through an approach that drew upon both inductive and deductive coding constructs. Deductive coding constructs were drawn from current literature focusing on both short-term and long-term effects of the pandemic, and on higher education more broadly. Such codes included pedagogical change, alterations to student and teacher experiences, and the awareness of equity concerns among college students. Inductive codes arose from the data itself. A complete copy of the survey can be found in Appendix C. Next, the chapter features findings from the interviews with two faculty developers as well as results from the faculty survey distributed at River Junction Community College.

FACULTY DEVELOPMENT
IN A TIME OF UNCERTAINTY

Southeast Valley Community College

Michael Jacobs began our conversation about faculty development in a time of uncertainty by recounting the start of the pandemic in mid-spring 2020. This recounting was almost a moment-by-moment, day-by-day retelling of the occurrences. Many faculty members remember the distinct transition that institutions faced in mid-Spring 2020, and Michael's retelling captures both the personal and the professional:

> Interestingly enough, it was Friday the 13th. That's when everything really hit. I was in Jacksonville. I had driven down to Jacksonville. I taught that Thursday, and since I'm on the coast, I surf. I loaded my board, went down to Jacksonville, and had a workshop in Jacksonville for a trade school, an aviation maintenance trade school. Got back from Florida where I did my workshop, came back, and we didn't have class Monday. We were "off," we were told by our administration. Administration canceled class and immediately said that we were going to move fully online and gave us that week to prepare.
>
> I am part of a team now that is a professional development [PD] division. Before that, we did not have a PD division. I was the only person. Now we have an executive director over PD, staff, and faculty. And then we have me, who's the director of faculty development. We, as a team, got together and put together a manual to help people to move their classes online. We put together a series of trainings where we provided direction for using Skype because we did not have MS Teams yet. Those were mandatory for faculty to attend. We did the same training five times, and it lasted ninety minutes. It was also recorded and accessible. I don't know how they handled who didn't and did not attend, who did or did not attend.
>
> That's what we did. We did that. Provided one-on-one assistance when needed. I was given responsibility for one campus and this campus is relatively small. The rest of the team handled the main campus and the other three campuses, so they handled more questions.

Michael's words captured how higher education was no longer simply being asked to change. Change was forced upon higher education. Faculty development directors, like Michael, became the meditators between the faculty and the external circumstances that prompted the need for change, and faculty developers had to quickly assess what pieces of teaching online were most needed at a time when all faculty would be asked to make the transition to teaching online. What were the most essential and critical pieces that faculty needed?

In his role as faculty development director, Michael described how, in mid-spring 2020, he aimed to provide faculty with baseline knowledge about the learning management system they used at Southeast Valley, D2L (formerly Desire2Learn). While he knew that most faculty knew the basics of D2L, such as grades and attendance, he also knew that faculty who did not teach online were not held to the same standard as those who had used D2L to teach online. Michael said, "If you teach online at our institution, then you're held to a very different standard [than those who teach face-to-face]. You are required to be active and engaged. There's different levels of that, of course, but you are expected to not just load documents and have midterm and final."

The pandemic changed this as there would no longer be two distinct faculty groups according to modes of teaching (those who teach face-to-face and those who teach online) and Michael noted that he was just trying to get faculty—mostly those who had not previously taught online—used to using D2L for more than grades and attendance. He said, "We were just trying to get people to use what's in D2L. There was nothing extra. We didn't talk about Nearpod or any apps. It was just like, 'Let's go over the basics. Content. Are you low content? How do you use the discussion forum? How do you use the quiz tool?' Very basic, and focusing entirely on our LMS."

Michael also discussed several courses that contained hands-on components that were difficult to put online. Yet, he described how faculty moved everything online as best as they could. In mid-spring 2020, labs were moved online and instructors became creative, finding videos of labs in their subject areas and even encouraging students to simulate labs of their own, especially in areas where they could collect specimens on their own. Students received credit from those labs as they would have if the course had continued to meet face-to-face.

Michael's recounting of the transition that faculty had to make was one that stressed continuous flexibility and adaptation. By summer 2020, he noted that small groups of students were coming onto campus for specific subjects such as welding and machine tool technology. There were also programs, like golf course management and culinary arts, that required internships, and some of those were able to occur.

Yet, as Michael described how leadership was grappling with future semesters, he said, "We're probably going to continue in a similar manner as we have. We have not really been given definitive answers. We're in a holding pattern right now." Michael's characterization of continuing to move forward despite being in a holding pattern encompassed the idea that his campus would continue making the choices it deemed possible to make while mitigating the risk of meeting face-to-face.

The delay in decision-making was starting to take a toll on Michael and faculty at Southeast Valley Community College. Michael's frustration emerged when he described the uncertainty that hung over the fall 2020 semester. The uncertainty affected not only faculty, but students. Michael said:

> Here's the thing that's a problem. We have these classes out there that are available for students to register in but I really know that in the end they are going to be moved online. And the students don't know yet. They are signing up for face-to-face but it will be online. This is bad planning. I feel like they [the administration] should have made a decision months ago. I feel like they should have said, "Some classes that are now scheduled for face-to-face may move online. And those may be synchronous online classes. There's a lack of leadership.

Mentioning synchronous online teaching prompted Michael to further discuss shifting formats of teaching, noting that most online teaching at Southeast Valley was asynchronous. Noting that it was difficult for the administration to make synchronous online learning a viable form of instruction, Michael claimed he would love to see more synchronous online classes, but it just might not be feasible.

Michael also discussed HyFlex teaching. HyFlex, a course format and instructional approach that combines face-to-face and online learning, with students able to choose if they want to take the course in-person, synchronously online, or asynchronously online, has become much more popular as a result of the pandemic. Michael noted that though instructors have the ability to enact HyFlex teaching now, it likely wouldn't be done well.

When asked whether this might be a useful or valuable strategy for some instructors, Michael noted that synchronous online learning would be most helpful for students. He also noted the challenges that many students face who have little access to high-speed internet or a laptop. Students were sometimes in the position of having to write papers by hand and take pictures of them or use a word processing program on their phone. Southeastern Valley, he noted, had a limited number of laptops that they loaned to students about a month into the pandemic in spring 2020.

At the close of our discussion, Michael was quick to offer an addendum to his previous comments about administrative decisions, saying, "But I do feel bad for our administrators. They've never done anything like this before. I can complain about the lack of communication or decisions that are not being made, but they're in a tough bind. I have sympathy and compassion for them, for sure." The theme of faculty developers being beholden to administrative decision-making shaped Michael's commentary on his ability to work with faculty in unprecedented times. How administrative decisions impacted faculty and students alike was high on his list of concerns. There was a strong sense that the pandemic had made an already multicampus community college more decentralized, so Michael saw his role as director of faculty development as critical in working with the faculty on the campus to which he was assigned.

Desert Plains Community College

Annette Hansen was eager to present an overview of the Center for Teaching and Learning (CTL) at Desert Plains Community College, one of the largest of ten community college branches in the Southwest state in which Desert Plains is located. Annette described her

CTL as being in existence for twenty years; its status was that it was the oldest CTL in the district. Annette's staff of ten employees who worked at the CTL was also a long-established group, with most of the employees having a longer history at the CTL than Annette.

The pandemic had forced the group to connect and work virtually. Annette noted that currently the only two members of her team that were working on campus were the multimedia team, and that was just for one day per week; faculty and staff at Desert Plains had been asked to stay out of campus buildings during the pandemic. Parking lots, administrators said, should be empty so employees could model the message of staying home to the community.

Reflecting on the start of the pandemic at Desert Plains, Annette claimed that she thought colleges needed to establish a strong digital presence early. She added, "and we've never had to do that before." Because of the high enrollment numbers at Desert Plains and the multiple branches, the institution had always been highly visible. But all of this changed in mid-March 2020. When asked what the first things were that happened at Desert Plains, Annette immediately responded, "the Desert Meet-Up."

Annette described the meet-up as an early intervention that sought to build community with faculty across campus and sustain that community in the early part of the transition to teaching fully online. For about six weeks, from mid-March to the beginning of May 2020, the Desert Meet-Up was an online drop-in space that met from 8–9 a.m., five days a week. The main goal of the meet-up was to foster connection. Each day in these early months of the pandemic, about 15–20 people gathered at the meet-up. There was no agenda and some people called in while walking their dogs or drinking their coffee. And IT (instructional technology) always came. Annette noted that by IT coming and supporting people's questions about technology, a culture was built that focused on responsiveness to the current situation, teaching and learning online.

After six weeks, just five people showed up to the meet-up and Annette claimed that the need was not there anymore. The meet-up had accomplished what it had hoped to accomplish: bringing people together and sorting through questions about how to move forward in an era in which teaching and learning were moved completely online. People felt connected after six weeks, knew who to talk to, and felt comfortable reaching out if they had questions. The meet-up was for everyone on campus, including staff and full-time and adjunct faculty.

Trainings for Webex, the video-conferencing tool that Desert Plains used as a platform for synchronous online teaching, were also held often in the early weeks of the pandemic. Every department had three scheduled trainings (morning, afternoon, and late afternoon) to accommodate all. Annette mentioned that these departmental trainings allowed participants to ask specific questions about Webex tools that were especially pertinent to their department. Adjuncts were also invited. Cranium Café, the other platform that Desert Plains used for advising and student services, allowed students to easily contact faculty or advisors in the moment and have their questions answered.

Annette reflected on the shift to serving students entirely through online platforms versus connecting through a physical presence on campus. Noting that the CTL has a central location on campus, Annette noted that they typically had a large amount of foot traffic, with people popping in to ask questions or talk between meetings. With Cranium Café, students or faculty can virtually "knock on each other's doors," a feature that allows some kind of virtual replication of the face-to-face setting. If someone is offline and has someone knock at their door, an email is sent to the person with a note that someone is trying to reach them. Some of these changes were gradual and gained traction over a period of weeks, through urging students and faculty to utilize the digital resources that were available to them.

Interestingly, Annette described how not going entirely online had been the biggest challenge for Desert Plains. She described the scenario for fall 2020 as consisting of offering four different types of courses at Desert Plains: 1) live online, 2) on your own time online, 3) hybrid, and 4) in-person. At first glance, defining each may seem doable; however, Annette noted that the consistency of use of particular platforms in one type of course versus another was not there. She said, "We do not, for example, define what percentage of class needs to be in-person to call it hybrid. It could just be the final exam [that is face-to-face]. Annette distilled the challenges she, as a faculty developer, experienced by asking a rhetorical question: "One of the biggest challenges is trying to navigate who's teaching what and how. And then [we ask] how we can best support faculty so their students can be successful."

Annette and her team, though they are a team of ten, quickly understood that it would be almost impossible for them to serve each faculty member on campus who had questions about the transition to teaching online. They identified course leads, or faculty members who took the lead in designing courses that had multiple sections. The course lead worked with the instructional design team to help design a course and then multiple sections of the course would be rolled out to adjuncts to teach, with some flexibility for tweaking each section. Annette noted that the assistance from course leads had been very helpful to both the faculty development team and to faculty themselves.

In reflecting on the flurry of change and transition undergone over a few short months, Annette was able to note the closeness she felt with faculty, staff, and others as a result of all of the work that they had done together online. She said:

> It's funny, my staff and I have been meeting every day since this started. We have a staff meeting every day for half an hour to an hour. And we are constantly marveling at how we honestly feel like we're a little bit more connected to faculty now than when we were on campus. You get comfortable where you walk at the college, and where you go to, and your space. But digitally, everybody's had to reach out for some sort of support on some level. And suddenly it's very easy for them to just knock on our door or pop in. And it's quite loved. I actually feel a bit more connected.

Though Annette mentioned that, at the start of the pandemic, the meet-ups were focused on check-ins and questions, she described how discussions became substantive in the online space as well. Specifically, she said,

> We've had some amazing conversations after the killing of George Floyd, and we've had those powerful conversations as a college as a whole and as departments. We've also been working with departments to facilitate conversations about race with them. But, when you have these conversations, you have to have video. When you're going to have these conversations, you need to have your video on and your microphone [on] because these have to be authentic conversations. We can't hide behind the technology when we have these talks. But they've been very powerful. And I feel like there's more conversation happening than usual.

Annette also looked back at the initiatives her CTL had most typically done with faculty over the years and characterized them as the scholarship of teaching and learning. However, she added that "they had gotten a bit lost the last semester." In saying this, it seemed that Annette was talking about SoTL projects being buried in light of more pressing faculty development concerns. Annette noted that typically faculty were encouraged to do some action research around a topic and these initiatives had included, for example, "diversity inclusion, flipping your classroom, culturally responsive teaching, and assessment. . . . Since this [the pandemic era] happened, basically all of those subjects are gone and it's about course design or moving online. The need now is to be as strategic as we can with the money that is available to be able to get the largest impact."

Annette's astute focus on reaching a large number of faculty members with the topics that were most needed at the time came through in her comments about moving forward with faculty development during the pandemic era. Annette's organization, including dividing up her team members to be liaisons to specific departments, spoke to her high level of commitment and organization. This liaison approach, as she called it, has helped her foster conversations with individual faculty members, and faculty are starting to become more comfortable with the transition and situation they find themselves in. As Desert Plains move forward in supporting faculty in all four course formats, Annette has learned that reaching out to individuals and supporting conversations about innovation are the best ways to foster effective professional development for faculty.

River Junction Community College

The survey distributed to faculty at River Junction Community College provided the opportunity to include faculty perspectives in the understanding of the changes and challenges of faculty development during the pandemic era. Much like the faculty developers featured in this chapter, faculty themselves had to make rapid adjustments and just-in-time decisions to best serve their students. Faculty voices reflect a time of overwork, burnout, and isolation, but also reflect growth and optimism about the future of their teaching and a deepened compassion for students.

Many faculty members who responded to River Junction's survey about their perceptions of teaching during the pandemic year reported that the pandemic era's shift from face-to-face to online teaching required unprecedented amounts of time and energy. "Creating all my own digital content took hundreds of hours," wrote one faculty member. Indeed, well before the pandemic hit, a 2017 study found that teaching online is more time-consuming than teaching in person (Grove, 2017). Undoubtedly, the task of moving content online was even more challenging for faculty who lacked experience in online teaching.

One respondent to River Junction's survey expressed empathy for colleagues who did not have prior online teaching experience. This respondent noted: "I've been teaching online for years. I knew the tools. I cannot fathom the transition for those faculty that were 100% face-to-face and minimal users of [the LMS]." This sentiment was often manifested in the real experiences of novice online teachers. One faculty member wrote: "I had to work three times as hard to transition face-to-face to an online platform. This is especially true since I had absolutely no training in how to do it."

Even those faculty members with online experience faced challenges in converting their face-to-face courses to online on short notice in the middle of the semester. Faculty were notified of the shift on March 13, 2020, and had a short, two-week timeframe to convert their courses (in addition to spring break, when faculty are off contract, faculty were given one extra week to complete the process). In response to this transition, one faculty member reported: "I did feel rushed. Although the college has provided a lot of training and resources, much of those resources came too close to the time my syllabus was due and classes were starting, so I didn't have time to learn it and apply it as I would have liked. I also felt I needed to become a web designer."

Faculty repeatedly expressed that time and effort to make the shift to online teaching was required; but faculty's dedication and frustration became almost palpable when reading their own words. "I have never worked so hard in all my life. I have never spent fifteen hours a day trying to do a single job," wrote one faculty member. Another wrote, "I spent hours over a two-week period learning new technology that was not required for a face-to-face class. As an adjunct, I did not receive compensation for any of that time." Similar perspectives from many were expressed over and over:

- "I made myself available nearly 24/7 to accommodate student needs."
- "I spent hours and hours working on trying to make the online course meet the richness of a campus course. I still don't think it went well."
- "I spent *so much* more time preparing for class."
- "[I was] exhausted and fatigued at the end of the day more so than when on campus."
- "With online classes, I feel like I'm on call 24/7."
- "It has been a herculean task for me to move online two courses that have *never* been taught online in the history of the college."
- "You cannot just take [face-to-face] materials, flip a switch, and suddenly have them come out as online materials. It requires a very different approach."

- "I had to make myself even more readily available above and beyond my normal, [even though] I'm usually very liberal in giving my time to students."
- "More was required of me as an instructor to help students. I was very challenged throughout this process."
- "To be effective, I found I needed to put in about three hours more per class in the online format."
- "It is not possible to keep standards and expectations up for students in this environment without working about 150% [above] 'normal' delivery."

This "Herculean" effort inevitably took a toll on faculty and caused River Junction Community College faculty members to experience "[i]ncreased workload leading to mental exhaustion and technological fatigue." Such feelings were consistent with teachers at all grade levels, as the pandemic placed an unprecedented workload on teachers (Kaufman & Diliberty, 2021).

A study conducted at the Yale Center for Emotional Intelligence found that American educators now "report extreme and prolonged stress" because of the pandemic, which can have long-term emotional and physical health repercussions (Brackett et al., 2020). Many faculty from River Junction reported feeling burned out and exhausted, including exhibiting both mental and physical symptoms. "There was an overwhelming amount of material to prepare every week. The stress caused physical symptoms in my body and I was unable to sleep and had a lack of appetite, for example," wrote one faculty member. "With so much extra work, it was hard to find time to relax. I worked into the evening most days," wrote another.

Another faculty member wrote:

I have not worked so hard for so long since graduate school. From May 2020 to October 2020, I did not take a single day off of work. It was unsustainable, and I felt continually burnt out. I felt like I did nothing but work on [the LMS] most of my waking hours, and that's horrible. And that's the thing, right? I don't feel like I'm spending that time helping students or teaching or what have you. . . . It really feels like the death of a thousand cuts having to check this box and enter those dates and fiddle with the html, etc.

The work during this era impacted not only the faculty at River Junction but the families of faculty members. One faculty member who noted this wrote: "I maintained my service to the college, my teaching rigor, my grading schedule. However, maintaining my role as a faculty member came at a cost to myself and possibly my family." Another faculty member who was also a parent busy arranging remote homeschooling for young children wrote: "This is not sustainable." Many others expressed similar challenges. For example, one faculty member wrote: "I'm exhausted. Doing all work via Zoom and email is never ending. There are fewer boundaries on my time and trying to manage kids learning from home while doing all of this has been nearly impossible."

In addition to the overwhelming increase in workload, feelings of isolation contributed to faculty burnout and mental well-being. Approximately 50% of respondents reported that the experience of transitioning to online teaching during the pandemic affected their mental health either significantly or very significantly. One respondent wrote: "I sought mental health therapy, [which] I had never had to do previously." Another faculty member said:

This year has been isolating. I miss the casual interactions with my colleagues. I miss being able to interact with my students. Home life and work blend together because it all occurs in the same space and time has lost meaning. There is much more stress and fewer opportunities for stress relief. There are good days and bad days—and the bad days are rough.

Reduced satisfaction in the job and a lost sense of joy emerged as themes in the survey responses. "The joy of interacting with students in class, which energizes and encourages me, was diminished," wrote one faculty member. This loss was felt not just in the classroom but in the job as a whole: "I miss just learning from my colleagues in the hallways. Online meetings get work done, but there's no real joy in them," wrote another faculty member.

Adjunct faculty at River Junction Community College seemed to feel especially isolated during the pandemic era. Many reported feeling less connected, as though they had been left on their own to figure things out. One adjunct faculty member noted: "As an adjunct, our interactions with others in our department [were] rare to begin with; now, interactions are virtually nonexistent. It is as if quarantining has gone virtual and not just physical."

The effects of burnout and isolation on faculty mental health are likely to be "long-lasting and pervasive" (Schroeder, 2020). One faculty member lamented: "My life has been turned upside down. Going forward, I will not be the same person, the same professor, I was before. The pandemic has changed the world and it has changed me, too."

But, despite the many challenges, the pandemic experience seemed not to be all doom and gloom; many River Junction Community College faculty reported that the lessons learned during the transition to online teaching invigorated their pedagogical methods and increased optimism about their teaching. Although 42% of faculty reported that they lowered their expectations for their students (e.g., showing flexibility for deadlines and attendance, trimming course content to ensure students got what they most needed, etc.), 53% noted that they had increased their expectations for themselves (e.g., one faculty member wrote: "I had to learn a new way to teach after twenty years and I love it, so I pushed myself so much more"). Another faculty member described the shift in expectations this way: "In order to lower the expectations for my students, I had to increase the expectations of myself to better cater to the different learning needs of my students."

And while 58% of survey respondents indicated that creating a sense of community in the online classroom was the most challenging aspect of the transition to entirely online teaching, it became readily apparent in comments that many faculty members used this challenge for growth and innovation. Several noted that they will carry this growth into future classroom settings, whether virtual or face-to-face. One faculty member wrote that this challenge "was hard for me, as a perfectionist. But I had to give myself space to learn. I asked my students to keep telling me what they needed, and they kept telling me I was doing fine. I think they were overly kind."

In fact, many teachers viewed the transition to online teaching as an opportunity to update their teaching methods. Some had intended to do this but had not accomplished it yet. One faculty member wrote: "I have wanted to put everything online for my [face-to-face] class for years. This made it happen. But it has also shown me that there is no replacement for quality [face-to-face] interaction with students." Another faculty member wrote: "I like the redesign of my courses and am glad I was forced to alter them." Some faculty members believed that the pandemic had accelerated opportunities for development and change that are inherent in good teaching. In particular, one survey respondent wrote:

> I believe that this time was significant for forcing me to adapt to and utilize all types of technology and techniques for delivering content to students that was graspable and memorable. We, as teachers, are always trying to improve our lessons and find more ways to make the knowledge stick and help our students grow. This experience forced us towards a certain path, but the growth mentality has always been there.

The changes that faculty were forced to make during the pandemic transition from face-to-face to online instruction gave faculty more tools to increase student engagement. Perhaps complacency, lack of awareness, or lack of time prevented some faculty from implementing innovative pedagogical practices (e.g., scaffolding, experiential learning, metacognition, etc.) that are known to be effective for today's student. Some reactions from respondents to the survey put things in absolutes:

> I'm never teaching a three-times-a-week lecture class ever again. I'm teaching [ongoing] hybrid classes that meet once a week for an

extended period and have more reading/source use outside of class
that we discuss when we meet.

The shift away from lecture was cited often by respondents to the
survey. One faculty member noted: "I will focus much more [on]
in-class discussions rather than straight lecturing." Another faculty
member reported that he will add "more activity-based learning
rather than lecture-based learning." Some faculty plan to improve
student engagement by reducing lecture and adding "more in-class
activities. . . . I will try to involve the class in short one-on-one
meetings that generally try to make the learning experience more
conversational."

In addition to making class more "conversational," the value of
experiential learning has become more apparent during the pandemic era. Faculty noted that less class time was spent on things
students can do on their own outside of class. Fewer lectures meant
that students had to be more responsible for reading material and
viewing digitally recorded lectures on their own; therefore, more
time was left for hands-on learning.

The potential benefits of HyFlex, an instructional approach that
combines face-to-face and online learning, with students able to
choose if they want to take the course in-person, synchronously online, or asynchronously online, have also been highlighted. One instructor planned to allow "students to Zoom into the class if they are
physically unable to make it to class (when needed—not just when
they don't want to come to class)," while another faculty member
planned to "record a class time on Zoom if a student needs to miss
class—or perhaps allow a student to attend via Zoom if he or she
can't attend in-person for a very good reason."

The theme of allowing more flexibility with class attendance was
common across the survey responses; as the technology for HyFlex
classrooms continues to evolve, the method may become more
widely accepted and implemented as a result of these experiences.
One faculty member noted: "Development of a new course into a
virtual format will continue in order to create online offerings. I

think faculty will choose more hybrid formats in the future so they can mix the benefits of some [face-to-face] with some virtual tools. I think we will see fewer [face-to-face] format only classes."

Faculty are considering ways to continue providing flexible options for students. One faculty member noted: "I will continue to offer Zoom as an option for all students when they are unable to attend class. If they are sick, have a doctor's appointment, etc., and would not be able to come to campus but still can Zoom, I will remain flexible. My goal is for students to participate in class. The mode in which they participate is not important."

Maintaining academic integrity, particularly for testing, was an issue and concern for faculty at River Junction Community College. During the transition to being fully online, faculty members engaged in sometimes heated discussion about the benefits and drawbacks of using lockdown browsers, cameras on students, and/or requiring in-person testing during the pandemic. These concerns came through in the responses to the survey questions.

One faculty member wrote about testing by saying: "It's impossible to maintain integrity and there isn't support from the college right now on this. I really feel like the college can do more in the proctor/testing area and give more flexibility to students in taking online courses with in-person testing. If a course needs in-person testing to hold the class to the standards of excellence, that's how it must be." The current debate about testing was ongoing throughout higher education, and another faculty member noted, "eradicating cheating is nearly impossible with how quickly technology is moving."

Instructors were now being encouraged to rethink the traditional ways of testing students and work on developing and designing new kinds of assessments that deter cheating (Millward, 2020). It is evident in the survey responses that faculty members explored new approaches. One instructor noted that he planned to offer "fewer multiple-choice tests and more reflections and presentations by students" as a way to assess student learning, while another wrote: "I will require students to write quiz reflections. I stopped grading quizzes during this time, which is why I started requiring the reflections. I'm not sure if I will grade quizzes again, but I know I will require the reflections."

Another faculty member equated these new strategies with having more care for students and described a change in assessment practices: "I've increased the use of formative and other assessments in Canvas as well as increased use of simulations and third-party website tools to help students practice with various material. I also am much more aware of the well-being of my students and try to communicate much more affirmatively and promptly with students."

In fact, despite the burnout and overwork, increased compassion for students was a repeated theme seen throughout the survey responses. Viewed through the lens of faculty's demonstrated exhaustion and stress, the concern that faculty also expressed for their students was perhaps surprising, but inspiring. In response to the question: "What changes have you made in your teaching that will continue once we are 'back to normal?'", one faculty member put it succinctly yet powerfully by stating: "Expressing more kindness." Another provided a subtle yet eloquent response: "I became very patient."

Others echoed this sentiment, including one respondent who wrote: "I kept being a cheerleader and was flexible. . . . I knew the transition and the pandemic itself was stressful and I wanted to make the transition as smooth as possible. . . . I made an effort to help my students with their individual needs and also to accommodate their new and changing realities."

Faculty perceived that this increased empathy would improve the classroom environment. "I have adopted some new policies to make my classes less stressful on students, and overall, I really like the positive impact it has made on my class environment," wrote one faculty member. Another stated, "I start every online class with a good news check-in to create community. I will do that in the classroom in the future as well."

The flexibility and self-direction that such changes required were evident in instructors' observations of how their classrooms had changed. One faculty member stated: "I had to get comfortable allowing students to get by with some things that I normally would not [have], given the challenges they faced due to the pandemic. So, I became more empathetic than usual at the expense of academic rigor. That seemed appropriate."

Equity issues among students were also a concern, with faculty taking into account students' access to technology and reliable internet access and how this might influence future classroom settings. One survey respondent wrote: "I will definitely do a survey early in the semester to find out what kind of technology my students have and steer them to campus resources that can help them." Others reported increased empathy for students who were "doing the whole class on their phone." Faculty noted the need for understanding and working with the limitations of students.

Finally, and especially relevant to the focus of this book, it is important to consider the effects of the pandemic era on collaboration within the college. One of the survey questions asked about this very directly: "What new collaborations have you seen at the college as a result of Covid-19?" Some faculty reported that they did not see much collaboration, with several replying "N/A" or "None." The theme of isolation discussed above reinforces this perception. Several of the responses about collaboration were as follows:

- "None. I've been working from home most of the damn time in my own silo."
- "I really felt isolated, so I think there was very little collaboration!"
- "I have witnessed no new collaborations."
- "I personally haven't seen any."
- "I have witnessed no new collaborations."

Others responded similarly to this question; however, analyzing individual responses within the context of the data as a whole painted a different picture. Faculty told story after story that illustrated many rich and unprecedented collaborations that took place during the pandemic transition. New collaborations and collegiality within the department were common, as the following response illustrates:

In the spring of 2019, my department got together many times on Zoom to share ideas of what worked or didn't work. This was extremely helpful! Plus, it was encouraging to talk to my colleagues, whom I hadn't seen in person for quite a while. We don't normally have time for this kind of dialogue so that was a benefit of all of us teaching online and being at home.

Collaborations within departments were mentioned repeatedly. For example, one response noted that "department faculty joined forces to share/create content for some of the in-person to virtual class transitions," while another noted "[W]ithin my specialty area, we now meet weekly and chat, which has been amazing in that it allows us to split up work and share our ideas." Another respondent wrote, "More of my department is using Teams and Zoom. We've set up a social hour once a week to be able to have some sort of community."

New collaborations were also evident across disciplines. One faculty member mentioned faculty development workshops, noting the value of "discussions with cross-discipline colleagues about teaching best practices during PDD (Professional Development Day) sessions." Many others observed the increased dedication to students' needs, and this was shared among colleagues regardless of discipline. One faculty member wrote: "I've seen more teachers helping other teachers figure out how to engage students online."

There were instances of individuals helping each other, and one respondent wrote: "I worked with another instructor from a different program to help her develop new career training for her students." The shared realization of the importance of joint work was a uniting factor. Another instructor pointed out: "Colleagues across the campus are passionate about the quality of teaching."

Collaborations not only occurred across academic departments, but with other campus services. The college's Educational Technology Center (EdTech) was heavily relied upon during the transition from face-to-face to online instruction, and many strongly expressed appreciation. "EdTech has been an amazing resource! The staff have been so patient during the transition," wrote one instructor. This enthusiasm came through in several respondents' comments: "EdTech has been vital to my success and sanity!" Another instructor wrote: "I can't say enough about the accessibility and assistance provided by everyone in EdTech. I wouldn't have survived without them."

Faculty appreciated other campus departments as well. "There are lots more connections with various departments on campus and more interactions around offering services for students," one instructor noted. Student Services also provided support, and one instructor described how they came into classes virtually and provided all remote students opportunities (Zoom lectures, Kahoot activities, sending welcome bags to homes, etc.).

The library was often cited as an essential resource, including the practice of embedding librarians in online course shells to support students. The virtual classroom allowed for more visiting lecturers, as well. One respondent said, "I have invited a lot of guest speakers to help break up the monotony and bring fresh perspectives." Another said, "Speakers have become more important for classes entirely online or hybrid as this allows for students to understand real industry perspectives when live tours are unavailable."

Faculty also expressed appreciation for the support and resources the college provided for students. Many relied on "Early Alert," a reporting mechanism for when a teacher becomes aware of a student having personal, financial, or academic issue. As a part of the "Early Alert" process, a counselor, student engagement ambassador, or academic achievement staff member contacts the student about available support resources. Instructors were also able to direct their students to extra resources that were provided for students during the pandemic. One respondent said: "The laptop rental program has been crucial. At least half a dozen of my students were able to complete their classes due to the resources provided by that initiative."

Even the time-honored faculty versus administration rivalry seemed to have subsided during this time of crisis. The comment that "The college administration has been stellar in their response to the pandemic crisis," perhaps expresses a level of appreciation that administration does not often expect to hear from faculty. "I appreciate college administrators' efforts to verbalize their thanks and gratitude to faculty for stepping up and doing whatever was needed to keep classes moving forward," wrote one instructor. Another faculty member summed it up this way:

> River Junction Community College did an excellent job of being proactive in the pandemic in all sorts of ways—from closing down school immediately to initiating precautions upon return, communicating with the students and staff consistently throughout, providing faculty with the tools to adapt quickly to online learning and then enforcing that with an online class introducing us to those technologies, and most importantly, reaching out with mental health and other resources to help those in need. There was not a thing they did not think of.

While the pandemic era was isolating and stressful, it was evident that faculty members at River Junction rose to the challenge to best teach their students; and, despite the challenges, they found innovative and supportive ways to collaborate in doing so.

During this era, there was much discussion about the changes the pandemic era brought to higher education. Perhaps one change that will be sustained is that struggling through this trying time would ultimately lead to a breaking down of traditional silos and hierarchies to encourage more collaboration. As one faculty member reflected: "The realization that we are all in this together—I think that ended up being a significant force for creating cohesion." Although colleges and universities currently face many challenges, fostering such cohesion and collaboration among departments, faculty, and staff will strengthen the institution of higher education.

COLLABORATION IN A TIME OF UNCERTAINTY

Chapter 3 featured faculty development before the first full pandemic year and how both SoTL and FLCs resonate with faculty-led faculty development, emphasizing that the best faculty development is faculty-led faculty development. This chapter, in contrast, depicts how faculty development needed to shift in the pandemic era. This chapter focuses on how faculty development was focused almost exclusively on presenting faculty with the tools they needed to be successful in the online space. Similar to how faculty development was fostered pre-pandemic, successful faculty development during the first full pandemic year was built upon collaborative work between faculty developers and faculty. Next, this chapter frames these findings through tenets of collaboration theory.

As previously noted, collaboration is a process that occurs over time and is manifested in "personal relationships, psychological contracts, and informal understandings and commitments" (Thomson & Perry, 2006, p. 22). Faculty developers Michael Jacobs and Annette Hansen reflected on the early days of how their institutions addressed the changes brought about due to the pandemic, and it became clear that the uncertainty of the situation circulated feelings of uncertainty across institutions.

Both Michael and Annette wondered if they would be able to effectively alter operations successfully and assist faculty with meeting new challenges. Michael and Annette gave several nods to flexibility and adaptation that signaled the ever-changing situation that institutions experienced in spring 2020. The dimensions of collaboration theory, manifested in the work of faculty developers during the early days of the pandemic, assist us in understanding the nature of how faculty developers needed to adapt.

Faculty themselves, as illustrated through the survey responses from River Junction Community College, were the on-the-ground implementers of changes in teaching. Such work caused faculty to have mixed feelings of struggle, isolation, and growth. It was clear that the majority of faculty felt that the learning curve they had in translating face-to-face courses to the online space was challenging. Despite this, faculty experienced collaborative realities during this era. Next, the chapter highlights how the dimensions of collaboration shifted within this new era, manifesting themselves in different ways than they had pre-pandemic.

Governance

The governance dimension of collaboration emphasizes that there must be structure within collaboration. For governance to work among participants, participants must be willing players in the work. Faculty developer Annette Hansen's discussion of how such governance was operationalized in the pandemic era became clear as she discussed how her leadership supporting faculty felt thwarted by department chairs and other administrators.

Annette described how she needed to shift her work and leadership as a faculty developer when the pandemic removed her from the physical space of campus. Specifically, Annette noted how the Center for Faculty Learning (CTL) was a hub of activity before the pandemic and a meeting place of sorts. When the pandemic forced everyone to work from home, no longer were physical meetings a bridge to connecting with faculty. Annette lovingly described how faculty would often need to cross the CTL as they walked across campus due to its central location. Many conversations sprung from informal meetings. Annette had to brainstorm how to effectively implement an "open office door" in the virtual space and described many successful initiatives, such as the Desert Meet-Up, that emerged as a way to effectively govern in the virtual space.

Annette also noted that because physical meetings were no longer possible, she had to brainstorm new ways to reach her constituents, the faculty. She said:

> You know, it's really interesting. At the start of the summer, I had been reaching out to department chairs and asking if faculty are interested in doing this [a workshop on a particular topic]. I consistently had two department chairs say, "My faculty are on break. Don't ask them." But, at the same time, I was getting emails from faculty asking for this or that. And I thought this was a bit incongruent. The chairs are trying to protect them, which is appropriate. But we are trying to offer opportunities.

Annette described how she was able to essentially change the governance structure by becoming a liaison. Instead of going to department chairs and asking whether faculty wanted to participate in workshops that she and her office were offering, she went directly to faculty. She said, "When we [faculty developers] email individual faculty and ask them if they are interested in workshops about particular topics, they often answer with excitement [and say] that they want to participate."

Such an approach led to more conversation and communication with faculty. When Annette was getting "shut down," as she described it, by departments and department chairs, she noted that she could not tell if the response she received was really from faculty not wishing to participate or was coming only from the department chair. Annette mentioned that faculty developers, as a result of being pushed aside, began to question why they were pursuing what faculty needed through the typical governance structure instead of one that felt more collaborative with faculty themselves. Collaboration with faculty themselves generated new possibilities and created a new governance structure for faculty development in a new era. Connecting with the faculty was a definite plus in an era of uncertainty.

Administration

Annette's pursuit of collaboration, described above, also touches on the administration, or administering, dimension of collaboration. The typical top-down structure of people at the top (i.e., department chairs, as noted in the example above) making the rules and then instructing someone to enforce them may be how most think administration works. But, as seen with the implementation of faculty development during the pandemic at Desert Plains, there may be more success in initiating change through operationalizing a horizontal structure to the administration dimension of collaboration. Because the pandemic had the effect of dispersing faculty and thereby made the organization more decentralized, Annette had better success reaching out horizontally to faculty as a way to gauge faculty's needs than working vertically through top-down channels.

Michael reflected on the role of administration throughout the first six months of the pandemic and remained skeptical. He questioned how much leadership administration could provide in the beginning of the pandemic when decisions seemed to be always delayed, pushing him to wonder how his institution would pivot when the time came for it to do so. He provided the example of course scheduling and how students were kept unaware of schedule changes that would ultimately affect them.

Michael repeatedly emphasized that the lack of leadership at Southeast Valley and the uncertainty about the future was casting doubt on the institution's ability to work through the challenges the pandemic presented. Unlike Annette, it did not appear that Michael felt he could initiate certain changes without being told what changes were needed. A horizontal dimension of the administration component of collaboration theory appeared to be lacking in Michael's position.

Even faculty at River Junction echoed a shift to more horizontal forms of administration. Left to problem-solve about how to translate their courses to the online space, faculty became more key in decisions about course delivery. As the ones closest to the student experience, faculty were on-the-ground implementers of change, and faculty were the ones to assess what was working with students and what was not. Some faculty even commented that the pandemic, as an external force, was what they needed to operationalize some of the changes in pedagogy that they had been intending to implement for some time. Clearly, many expressed that the learning curve was intense but that the push to change was worthwhile.

Autonomy

Faculty autonomy was something Michael Jacobs valued and spoke to, specifically when he mentioned that faculty were at vastly different places in using D2L, the online learning management system that Southeast Valley used for instruction. Michael had a good read on how particular faculty needed to come up to speed with online teaching, whereas others were fully competent in teaching online. One of the first actions Michael described at the start of the pandemic was the creation of workshops for faculty who needed to learn the basics of D2L.

As both faculty members and faculty developers, both Michael and Annette were cognizant that faculty needed to feel a balance between autonomy and working for the collective good. Many faculty they described already had a strong sense of how to move their classes online and function within a newly mandated format for instruction: teaching wholly online. Others, though, needed more assistance.

Both Michael and Annette mentioned how faculty who relied on hands-on components of classroom learning (for example, instructors who have students participate in labs) needed more guidance and ideas about how they might restructure their content into an online format. To foster autonomy, faculty had to have the tools to create and build their courses, and Michael and Annette were key contributors helping faculty attain these tools.

Faculty at River Junction had a desire to be autonomous and often reflected on the sheer amount of learning that they had done to adjust to online teaching. However, their efforts often had to be huge efforts, and many faculty reflected on how they were pushed to remain in a cycle of innovation and learning throughout the pandemic. In some cases, this led to faculty feeling overworked, and in others it led to feelings of isolation. Some expressed that learning fell primarily to them while others noted that the faculty development director at River Junction had been the main source of support for the shift to online teaching.

Mutuality

The mutuality dimension of collaboration theory points to how contributors perceive the actions they participate in with one another. Both faculty and faculty developers had a stake in how their institutions pivoted their instruction due to the pandemic. Michael noted how he was given the role of collaborating with one particular campus that was part of Southeast Valley. Through working with faculty at this campus, Michael noted that he carved out his role there as facilitator and mentor. He gave several examples of faculty whom he worked with, including one faculty member named Tom. Below, Michael notes how Tom and other faculty members he worked with learned new skills:

> We have a guy named Tom who has been at the institution longer than I have. He teaches golf course management. He's more of a botanist. He was really excited about teaching online because he was able to do some screen capturing and some recording, and then shared that with us as a team. He had learned these skills through someone else's professional development. I thought it was great how he was upbeat about using new tools in his teaching.

The sharing that occurred between faculty and faculty developers was an impetus for change as well as for fostering a sense of mutuality. New collaborations also came out of change. Michael, specifically, noted how interdepartmental collaborations came out of the era of the pandemic as well as more virtual collaborations. For these to continue, though, a sense of mutuality must be attained by both faculty developers and faculty alike. As instruction continued to pivot and respond to the pandemic throughout spring 2021, faculty developers needed to continue to gauge the needs of faculty—something that could not be anticipated a year earlier.

Though faculty at River Junction expressed concerns about increased siloing, they also gave a nod to increased mutuality, noting how departments banded together to consider ways of translating face-to-face classes to the online space. Support offered through the educational technology department and River Junction's libraries was also mentioned as facilitating collaboration and mutuality. Some respondents mentioned that departments had not only increased collaboration for professional and academic purposes, but had also initiated more opportunities for department conversation about a variety of issues.

Norms of Reciprocity and Trust

Reciprocity and trust are qualities that are never built overnight; instead, these dimensions of collaboration are fostered through working together as contributors toward a greater goal. Annette's long history with her institution as well as its sister college seemed to help her build reciprocity and trust with both faculty members and other administrators. Annette noted:

> I came here [Desert Plains] because, honestly, faculty respect faculty. And, so if you're going to talk to them about their teaching practice, you need to be faculty. And, in order to stay relevant and understand what faculty face on a day-to-day basis, you have to be part of the community, which means you have to be going to their meetings and you have to be part of the committees that they're on. And you can only really accomplish that if you are a faculty member. As a manager—when I had a role at another institution—I had to sit outside those roles. I had to meet with people to try and inform me, but I wasn't a member of the community.

Annette's keen observations helped her position herself as part of the faculty community and foster traits of reciprocity and trust with faculty. She was aware that this would create a bridge between her and faculty and help her be effective in working with them.

Faculty at River Junction vacillated between noting support from colleagues and identifying as primarily working in silos. Several faculty noted that their strength and perseverance came from building relationships with and supporting their students. And they noted that this is what kept them focused and ready to respond during the pandemic era.

TOWARD SYNTHESIS

Though the dimensions of collaboration theory, including governance, administration, autonomy, mutuality, and norms of reciprocity and trust, remained intact throughout the challenges the pandemic era presented, it was clear that faculty developers and faculty themselves needed to know how to alter the structures in place to serve their constituents—the faculty and students—effectively. Annette Hansen's and Michael Jacobs's work of reaching out to faculty directly and fostering networks with them despite a more decentralized campus stands as an example of an altered structure.

Mutuality became a more heightened dimension of collaboration as a result of the pandemic, pushing faculty developers and faculty alike to determine what the goals of the institution were and reaching out to serve students in new ways. Many faculty from River Junction noted that seeking support from fellow colleagues and focusing on the needs of students was the cohesion that was needed to make it through an uncertain, challenging era. Next, the final chapter explores what features of faculty development might remain the same and what aspects may shift after the pandemic era.

Chapter Five

Working Toward Collaboration in Faculty Development

Learning From Challenges

Collaboration theory illuminates how campus culture affects the implementation of any type of faculty development. The culture of an institution influences all the dimensions of collaboration, and changing the culture sometimes requires shifts in multiple dimensions of collaboration. As the previous chapter showed, though, sometimes radical shifts and new possibilities come about because campuses are forced to change. Taking into account the findings from all six case studies and how they relate to collaborative possibilities in faculty development at community colleges, this chapter elicits important considerations about the methods that drive faculty development within the community college context.

The book's central question is, In what ways can the implementation of collaborative faculty development within the community college promote improved pedagogical practices for faculty? This question shaped the ways in which collaboration within faculty development was conceptualized. Faculty development, and collaboration within it, intends to affect all three spheres of pedagogy: the teacher, the students, and the curriculum. Chapter 3 detailed three cases of how faculty developers implemented the SoTL and FLCs within their contexts, and chapter 4 focused on how the first full pandemic year prompted faculty developers to pivot—sometimes away from long-held initiatives like SoTL and FLCs—and articulate new priorities and new ways of engaging faculty.

Across the case studies featured in the previous chapters, faculty developers were united in their belief that collaboration benefits both faculty and the institution. Both before and during the pandemic, cross-disciplinary and cross-departmental connections gave faculty developers a broader picture of their respective institutions and allowed them to make decisions with faculty members that would benefit students across a spectrum of courses and programs. Faculty developers shared that faculty members who engaged in SoTL altered their teaching practices in some way, and those who participated in FLCs experienced enhanced collaboration with their colleagues. Enhanced collaboration improved faculty morale and affected the college culture.

Before the pandemic, community college faculty often lacked the time and resources to participate in faculty development focused on SoTL, and some institutions offered an incentive (such as a stipend) to faculty for participating. Because the sole job of community college faculty is to teach, and because the student population at community colleges represents a diverse cross-section of socioeconomic, ethnic, and racial groups, as well as students with different learning abilities, community college faculty are well-positioned within the academy to conduct SoTL research. It remains true, though, that community college faculty need additional time and resources to pursue SoTL.

Lack of time and resources was not the only impediment to community college faculty conducting SoTL and participating in FLCs, even before the COVID-19 era. The institutions themselves got in the way. As was illustrated in chapter 3, the hierarchical nature of academia can impede collaboration and growth. A lack of trust between faculty and administration can create tension that obstructs either side's ability to accomplish their goals. Ironically, both sides usually have the same goal—to offer the best services, opportunities, and education possible to students. Yet, the two groups sometimes were discussed by faculty developers as being at odds.

Sarah, the administrator from Northern Lakes Community College, discussed the benefits that arose from the cross-disciplinary connections that resulted from faculty's SoTL work. Sarah said, "Don't tell anyone, but [the opportunity for collaboration] is really what we're talking about here." Sarah was acknowledging that, while SoTL research itself is important, fostering greater collaboration as part of the campus culture was even more important.

If institutions of higher education can find ways to organize themselves to allow for a more heterarchical organizational structure—one that allows partners to share certain positions of power and authority equally—improved collaboration will result. Faculty will feel empowered to make decisions and choices that benefit the wider organization, and administrators will trust them to do so. Both partners must take responsibility for their own roles while also understanding their own and other roles within the organization. For this to happen, both partners must trust each other.

LESSONS FROM COLLABORATION

Thomson & Perry's (2006) five dimensions of collaboration theory include two that are structural (governing and administration); two that refer to social capital (mutuality and norms); and one that is agentive (autonomy). Together, these dimensions "signify collaborative action" (Thomsen & Perry, 2006, p. 24). The case studies featured in chapters 3 and 4 were anchored by the dimensions of collaborative theory. Viewed through the five dimensions of collaboration, the analyses of the interviews with faculty developers, as well as of the survey responses from River Junction Community College, highlighted the significance of particular dimensions that comprise effective collaboration.

For collaboration to be effective, the collaborating partners must "negotiate an equilibrium among the five dimensions that will allow them to achieve small gains in the short term, which will, over time, allow them to develop the trust and negotiated agreements necessary to realize longer-term benefits" (Thomsen & Perry, 2006, p. 29). Analyses of the cases conducted before the pandemic showed that the governing and administering dimensions were often solidified dimensions that had little room for negotiation or change. During the pandemic, however, shifts in governing and administering became possible due to new, more decentralized networks across campuses.

The governing dimension of collaboration theory requires that those seeking to collaborate must be able to make decisions jointly about how to govern behavior and relationships, and how to build processes for reaching agreement through shared power. Ideally, the governing structure should be nonhierarchical and allow for group consensus and openness in information sharing. Collaborative processes do not thrive in authoritative structures, but they are also not self-administering processes.

Collaboration presupposes the need or desire for achieving a purpose, and to accomplish that purpose, an administering or administration structure is necessary. This structure is what moves the process from governance to action. The "presence (or absence) of clear roles and responsibilities, the capacity to set boundaries, the presence of concrete, achievable goals, and good communication" are key for successful collaborative experiences (Thomsen & Perry, 2006, p. 25).

This second dimension of collaboration theory—the administration or administering dimension—was more malleable in the cases featured in chapter 4, collected during the pandemic era. The faculty developers featured in chapter 4 recognized they had a new role in recruiting faculty to collaborate with from afar. In fact, they knew they needed to be more purposeful about interacting with faculty and leading them.

Though the goal was still to create a space of learning and collaboration for faculty development activities, faculty developers, including Annette Hansen, featured in chapter 4, showed how they needed to be *conveners* of the process of collaboration. Annette had to find ways to directly engage with faculty about their needs and started doing that by directly asking faculty what their needs were.

Annette's action of circumventing department chairs and going straight to faculty to find out what their needs were is an example of how one faculty developer was able to find new ways to administer during challenging times. In doing so, Annette shifted the administering dimension of the process of collaboration at her institution.

Community colleges have always focused on the "localness" of their mission and the communities that they serve have always been central to their mission. Annette knew that she, as a faculty developer, needed to learn how community needs had changed; therefore, she had to go directly to faculty themselves in order to gauge the need to respond to the local. A time of crisis highlighted a need to move quickly to understand in which direction to pivot.

It is key that when parties come together to collaborate, they make choices that govern a variety of collective action problems implicit in joint decision-making—how to collectively develop sets of working rules to determine who will be eligible to make decisions; which actions will be allowed or constrained; what information needs to be provided; and how costs and benefits will be distributed (Ostrom, 1990). The context of the first full pandemic year became a launching point for possibilities in faculty development, as collective problems prompted joint decision-making. Annette's lament that the old governing structures were not generating solutions prompted her to take action in order to seek collaborative spaces for decision-making. The barriers of and lament about the old structure became a catalyst for change.

Without appropriate structure, though, it is difficult for humans to collaborate. Without humans, though, collaboration is impossible. It is not enough for collaborators just to share information. Without mutuality, collaboration cannot succeed. Mutually fosters interdependency, whether based on different or complementary interests, and is the foundation for effective collaboration.

Like the administering dimension of collaboration, the mutuality dimension became very strong during the case studies conducted during the pandemic. A shared interest in a common goal and a collective good was heightened when institutions were faced with new challenges. Therefore, the norms of this mutual reciprocity, along with trust (the belief among groups of individuals that another group behaves in good faith and with honesty), were fostered, especially between people who consistently shared common goals.

The "Desert Meet-Up," the initiative referred to in chapter 4 that was started by Desert Plains Community College at the beginning of the pandemic era, was an initiative that sprang into action to accomplish the goal of mutuality. As Annette Hansen noted, at the beginning of the pandemic, instructors and staff logged onto the Desert Meet-Up each morning, eager to just gather and share concerns about the new circumstance of teaching in a pandemic. Their shared concerns prompted a high level of investment in the dimension of mutuality. Six weeks into the pandemic, Annette noticed a shift. After six weeks, instructors had generally figured out how they were going to teach online and serve their students, and people had found informal and formal groups to connect with virtually for support.

The purpose of the Desert Meet-Up had been fulfilled and the structure was no longer needed in the form that it was first implemented in its five-day-a-week format. Desert Plains's ability to innovate and implement a structure at the start of the pandemic that served the needs of instructors and staff is an example of a responsive initiative that fostered greater mutuality among stakeholders.

The human factor of collaboration is, of course, a complicating factor. Participants in any kind of collaborative endeavor have a dual role wherein they maintain their own separate identity while simultaneously connecting with the collaborative identity. Participants in collaboration always experience a tension between self-interest and collective interest. This paradoxical autonomy can both hinder and enliven the collaborative process and must be managed effectively for productive collaboration to occur.

In terms of the dimension of autonomy, the participants featured in chapter 3 exhibited a heightened sense of autonomy in comparison to those featured in chapter 4. In the pre-pandemic context, it was evident that different institutions felt pride about particular aspects of their programs. Whether it was the length of time their CTLs had held SoTL workshops for faculty, or the depth of collaboration that existed between faculty and administration at their respective institutions, faculty developers featured in chapter 3 were clear about what their institutions were known for. This was a point of pride and discussion. And faculty developers were always striving to be known for something, always tweaking and remaking initiatives.

Faculty from River Junction also expressed a push–pull dynamic when it came to autonomy during the pandemic era. Several noted that changes to courses had to be done completely alone and in silos, while other faculty specifically praised the support of libraries and the technology support team at River Junction. Though the survey responses make it difficult to know whether autonomy was desired or whether faculty may have absolutely needed more support, it was clear that the shift to online learning necessitated a higher workload for most faculty. No longer could most faculty rely on tried-and-true versions of their face-to-face courses; instead, the external context of the pandemic era forced them to innovate and shift to a completely new teaching modality.

Before the pandemic, the autonomy that these institutions, faculty developers, and faculty exhibited was often thought of as unique; faculty developers and faculty alike were praised for their good ideas and these ideas were often what pushed them to collaborate effectively when they were sharing initiatives with each other. There was palpable enthusiasm from the faculty developers featured in chapter 3, as they were thrilled to participate in a focus group with each other and learn what different community colleges were doing with regard to faculty development. Each unique aspect of the SoTL and FLCs became a point of discussion and reflection.

Autonomy during the pandemic, though, became a central point of contention for many institutions, faculty developers, and faculty. The idiosyncratic ways of being and norms of different institutions sometimes impeded effective movement forward. Annette Hansen, discouraged at first with the hierarchical structure she experienced when she inquired with department chairs about what faculty members needed during the pandemic era, became an innovator as a result of structures at her institution that she perceived were stuck. Annette's reflection on how faculty development needed to change to be more responsive as a result of the pandemic was based on her recognition that new problems demanded new solutions. With this, she pursued more networked and interactive faculty development in the pandemic era than she had previously.

The cases featured in chapter 4 also began to display noticeable differences between how faculty developers and faculty talked about their work before the pandemic and during the pandemic. Before the pandemic, faculty developers relied on long-term, long-standing initiatives that could be adjusted and refined over time. As faculty developer Nancy said, there was pride that Eastern Shores Community College had been doing the SoTL with faculty for several years. A reliance on the history and longevity of faculty development initiatives was something Nancy claimed bolstered her institution's autonomy.

The pandemic vastly set any focus on long-term initiatives aside. No longer could faculty developers rely on long-standing initiatives; in fact, some faculty developers commented that SoTL had been, in a sense, set aside in early March and had not been picked up again for the rest of the spring semester. As a result of extreme changes that faculty developers had to face at the start of the pandemic, questions about student learning that did not involve changes due to COVID-19 became almost buried at some institutions.

Other institutions, such as River Junction Community College, had faculty members who expressed a desire to sustain long-term initiatives, such as SoTL, that were started before the pandemic. Such long-term initiatives became the place for faculty to step away from the fast-paced, problem-solving focus that faculty development had assumed in response to the pandemic. SoTL initiatives, in contrast, allowed for deep, in-depth considerations of teaching problems—some of which had intensified as a result of the pandemic.

Through sustaining its SoTL initiatives, River Junction reiterated a commitment to long-held tenets of quality faculty development, including its sustained and recursive process, while it also implemented faculty development focused on the pressing issues of the era. Faculty from River Junction felt, at times, grateful to be pushed toward innovation as a result of the pandemic. Some, noting that they had intended to innovate and revamp their teaching for years, noted that the opportunity had presented itself during the pandemic.

Pre-pandemic, faculty developers and faculty had a good sense of the conflicts and confluences of their individual roles within their institutions as well as of their collective roles. The governance and administration dimensions of collaboration were solidified, and faculty developers knew how they fit into the institutional culture and what ways they could make change with faculty. A mantra, repeated multiple times by all faculty developers, was "the best faculty development is faculty-led development."

Yet, faculty developers lamented that most faculty appeared to feel that they lacked the autonomy to take on governance roles; they perceived that they were subject to top-down directives from administration to participate in activities that they did not find meaningful. Viewed through the lens of collaboration theory, the theme of top-down versus faculty-led faculty development sometimes happened simultaneously.

In the cases collected during the pandemic (chapter 4), the concept of faculty-led initiatives became, in essence, a jointly created collaboration between faculty developers and faculty members. Topics that needed to be explored in faculty development (such as online teaching and learning) emerged through a genuine need and desire from faculty, and faculty developers were able to authentically facilitate these initiatives. The external force of the pandemic created a situation in which authentic collaboration between faculty developers and faculty led the way.

This focus on innovation and change resonates with what might be considered high-quality faculty development. If administrators desire that faculty participate and invest psychologically in faculty development activities, those activities cannot be perceived as being imposed upon them; rather, faculty development must be jointly arrived upon. But this shared power must go both ways. Faculty must also be willing to take ownership of their own faculty development, and the context of the pandemic presented faculty with a real need to pivot and inquire about their own teaching practices.

Before the pandemic, the hierarchical nature of most academic institutions created the perception that administrators held the power. This sometimes left faculty developers and faculty members feeling powerless as they felt obligated to participate in activities they did not find meaningful. However, if administrators are able to find a way to horizontally operationalize power as a way to release some level of control and allow faculty members to take share governance responsibilities, better collaboration will ensue.

This kind of jointly arrived upon collaboration will result in a broader understanding of each other's roles within the institution and a better understanding of the institution itself. Participants featured in chapter 4 indicated that a broader understanding between all stakeholders improves morale at the institution and ignites excitement among faculty. While this study does not attempt to address the impact on students of the improved morale caused by increased faculty collaboration, all participants stated an intuitive perception that students do, in fact, benefit when their teachers have this broader perspective.

One of the tenets of SoTL and FLCs is that they are voluntary opportunities; faculty have to volunteer to take part in such initiatives. Practically speaking, though, some systematic administration and coordination must take place if there is to be any systematic method to the collaboration and its outcomes. As discussed above, faculty themselves do not have the time to coordinate, communicate, organize, disseminate information, and keep partners apprised of the (ideally) jointly determined governance procedures. Yet, as also emphasized throughout the book, faculty prefer not to have a top-down structure to initiatives with an administrator enforcing mandates.

In the case of the participants in this study that were featured as part of the pre-pandemic context (chapter 3), each faculty member interviewed was granted release time from their teaching to administer the program. This is a solution to having both duties as a faculty developer and faculty member. Yet, each participant in this arrangement indicated that the release time was not sufficient to do either of their jobs as well as they would have liked; they lacked enough time to administer SoTL and FLC programming as effectively as they would have liked and they also felt that they did not have the time they needed to put into their classes.

Yet, according to the participants, if a faculty member or other person is given a full-time job as faculty developer, they are perceived as part of the administration and encounter the obstacles that arise from not being seen as a member of the faculty community. In short, in order to foster the most effective collaboration on a community college campus, solutions must be found to enable faculty developers to authentically and effectively work in both roles.

FACULTY DEVELOPERS' WORK: LOOKING TOWARD THE FUTURE

The results of faculty developers' work in the pre-pandemic context suggest that fostering effective collaboration across disciplines, across departments, and across the institution of the community college has many positive outcomes. It increases morale among faculty, can improve relationships between faculty and administration, benefits individual faculty members' growth as both teachers and learners, and has the potential of benefitting the student experience at each institution.

The phenomenon of siloing is known to exist in institutions of higher education. Even though most constituents and stakeholders are working toward the shared goals of serving students and improving education, they often work in isolation—in siloes. By working in this manner, stakeholders are not fully aware of the efforts of their colleagues in other areas of the institution. The pandemic era has exacerbated this siloing (sometimes referred to as isolation) among faculty further while at the same time pushing faculty toward new collaborative opportunities. The push–pull dynamic between the extremes of siloing and new collaborations has made the pandemic era one characterized by unique circumstances.

Those seeking to improve opportunities for collaboration should do so by focusing on managing and evaluating the five dimensions of collaboration: governance, administration, mutuality, autonomy, and norms of reciprocity and trust. As noted above, in fostering the process of collaboration, the governance dimension seems to be the most troublesome in the community college context. Collaborating partners need to be empowered to make decisions jointly to determine guidelines and desired outcomes.

This relationship should not be hierarchical, and both sides need to build trust. Faculty should be allowed the time and support to bring forth ideas and initiatives that promote their own development as well as better the institution. At the same time, faculty can be open to the ideas and initiatives brought forth by administration; for this to happen, administrators need to take the time to build relationships that foster reciprocity and trust, rather than forcing top-down mandates.

Since mid-spring 2020, faculty developers have been tasked with assisting faculty in moving courses to the online space. Faculty developers' role as pedagogical experts intensified during the early days of the pandemic, for they were the ones who campuses often turned to help faculty alter their pedagogy and effectively teach in the online space. Traditional faculty development has included seminars, workshops, and longitudinal programs but has not often focused on current rapid, on-demand, and self-regulated faculty development needs (Yilmaz et al., 2020). In the next section, this chapter articulates some of the distinct shifts that characterized faculty development in the uncertain era of the COVID-19 pandemic.

DISTINCT CHANGES FOR FACULTY DEVELOPERS AS A RESULT OF THE PANDEMIC

Yilmaz et al. (2020) articulate the type of faculty development needed in the future, given the dramatic shift seen in pedagogy in the current era. The first trend the authors discuss is just-in-time (JiT) faculty development. JiT focuses on a "need" in various formats and provides faculty with small amounts of content in order to meet ever-changing needs. JiT faculty development mirrors just-in-time learning, which people may be more familiar with, for the concept of just-in-time refers to engaging in information gathering when the need arises. Using one's smartphone to look up information on Google has propelled this kind of learning.

Similar to micro-credentials, JiT faculty development focuses on the perception that learning will be ongoing, but ever-changing, due to the context of learning needs. JiT faculty development was the mode of faculty development most drawn upon at the start of the pandemic as faculty developers were charged with assisting faculty in responding to an ever-changing pedagogical landscape.

As seen in the case studies featured in chapter 4, faculty developers became liaisons with faculty in order to figure out faculty's needs for JiT faculty development. Whether it was exposing faculty to the basics of the learning management system, as Michael Jacobs did in chapter 4, or translating laboratory work to the online space, JiT has become a go-to form of faculty development, one prompted by intense change and movement of courses to the online space.

The second theme of faculty development that Yilmaz et al. (2020) articulate focuses on performance analytics, thereby linking learning outcomes to faculty development. Creating faculty development programs that are effective in this way has not been the norm in faculty development, for pedagogical research debates the direct correlation between pedagogy and student outcomes. Faculty are often wary that analytics may further contribute to ever-increasing metrics that measure faculty effectiveness. At the same time, faculty development must be linked to increased student outcomes. Though there is plenty of evidence that faculty development initiatives are good for faculty, more must be done to link effective faculty development to improved outcomes for students.

Virtual communities of practice (VCoPs) are another way that faculty developers might respond to an environment that relies on increased online connectivity. Connecting geographically disparate faculty members is a possibility with VCoPs. Resonating with the tenets of faculty learning communities (FLCs), discussed in chapters 2 and 3, VCoPs offer the possibility of a collaborative space for faculty to participate in discussions about rapidly changing pedagogical practices. VCOPs happened naturally with the move toward online meetings. Yet, perhaps the tenets of FLCs can be more purposefully embedded in the online space, prompting the continuation of more in-depth, long-term initiatives such as the SoTL and FLCs.

Interactivity through online platforms became a goal that faculty developers increasingly embraced throughout the COVID-19 era. However, barriers to participating in faculty development have always included lack of time and logistics. Streaming video may help overcome these barriers by providing bite-sized content and participation at convenient times (Yilmaz et al., 2020). Like JiT faculty development, the online space can provide faculty with development opportunities tailored to their needs and schedule and perhaps deliver faculty development in new, more effective ways. Interactive video (perhaps using live polling or the chat feature) may promote faculty engagement with their learning, underscoring the need for faculty to be interactive participants in faculty development.

Finally, building capacity for teaching with technology is critical at a time in which many changes to teaching in higher education have occurred. Faculty developers must mentor all instructors in higher education to draw upon new teaching modalities, including online, hybrid, and HyFlex modalities. Faculty developers themselves must draw upon new technologies and harness them for creating new initiatives in which faculty will engage.

Across new kinds of faculty development, the concept of interactivity is stressed. Faculty must be invested in the issues and problems they inquire about. In many ways, the pandemic era ignited a mandate to adapt methods of teaching. Incorporating new modalities—primarily online modalities—into faculty development opened new possibilities for collaboration during an era shaped by uncertainty.

CONCLUSION

Continued innovation and focus on faculty development within the community college context has much potential. Faculty development has the power to influence, change, and improve faculty members' pedagogical practices. It also can allow instructors at community colleges to share the expertise they have developed in teaching a diverse student body with diverse needs.

Perhaps most importantly, faculty developers can promote opportunities for cross-disciplinary, cross-campus collaborations that benefit the institution as a whole. New collaborations, as ushered in during the pandemic era, have had both challenges and rewards for faculty. But faculty developers are those who may be able to step back and assess which aspects of faculty development must remain after the COVID-19 pandemic.

Will long-term initiatives like SoTL and FLCs continue to invigorate faculty? How can just-in-time faculty development offset the stress that faculty have felt concerning the shift in teaching modalities during the pandemic era? And how might changing administering structures promote more collaboration across administration and faculty structures? Such questions will remain on the table, and faculty developers must continue to negotiate their answers in relation to their respective community college contexts. Core to faculty development's mission is the concept that faculty can continue to learn and grow throughout their careers; the pandemic era underscored this reality.

Faculty developers can be key drivers of capacity building for teaching and learning in the community college context. Their knowledge of local contexts and of unique faculty and student needs will help their respective community colleges to adapt to new challenges. Improving teaching and learning while enhancing collaboration, has the potential to improve the experiences and performance not just of faculty members, but of every single member of the community college institution, from faculty to staff to students.

Appendix A

Semi-Structured Interview Questions for Interview and Focus Group Participants Featured in Chapter 3

1. Describe your institution. What is it like academically, physically, demographically, politically, culturally, etc.?
2. Describe your role in your position. What are your responsibilities regarding faculty development?
3. Describe the level of collaboration among faculty on your campus.
4. Describe the level of collaboration between faculty and staff on your campus.
5. How would you describe your level of familiarity with the scholarship of teaching and learning, or SoTL?
6. Can you describe how you first became aware of the concept of SoTL or FLCs? What was your initial reaction to these concepts?
7. In your own words, what is SoTL?
8. What level of familiarity do you believe your faculty has with the SoTL?
9. How do you incorporate SoTL principles into faculty development?
10. Describe your experience with faculty learning communities (FLCs).
11. How do you think participating in FLCs affects faculty morale?

12. How do you think participating in FLCs influences what faculty do in the classroom?
13. How effectively do FLCs foster collaboration?
14. What are the effects of collaboration on teaching effectiveness?
15. In what ways do you encourage faculty to improve their skills and methods in the classroom?
16. In what ways does collaboration among faculty affect the culture of the college?
17. In what ways does collaboration affect the way faculty members teach?
18. If you were to develop a fifteen-minute video introducing SoTL or FLCs for faculty, what might that look like? What would you want to be sure was included?
19. Describe successes you feel have come from offering FLCs.
20. Describe failures you feel have come from offering FLCs.
21. Can you draw any connections or conclusions to success, challenges, or changes at your community college as a result of faculty participation in FLCs?

Appendix B

Interview Questions for Participants Featured in Chapter 4

The following information was shared with participants before beginning interviews:

Mid-spring 2020 saw dramatic changes to the higher education landscape as a result of COVID-19. In a span of weeks, courses that had been face-to-face were moved to online spaces, using learning management systems such as Blackboard and Canvas. As universities addressed how to move residential students off campus in to comply with states' shelter in place orders, faculty were instructed to finish the courses they were teaching by putting all courses online. While some institutions touted this move as the greatest online teaching experiment for both K–12 schools and higher education, the deeper reality of online teaching during a crisis dominated this period in higher education. In an article entitled, "The Difference between Emergency Remote Teaching and Online Learning," authors Hodges et al. (2020) note that colleges and universities working to maintain instruction during such a time should understand that faculty "might feel like instructional MacGyvers, having to improvise quick solutions in less-than-ideal circumstances" and that teaching during this time is not online teaching, but rather *emergency remote teaching.*

1. Can you tell us about your role in faculty development during this time?
2. How did your role change and how is it still changing?
3. What was the most challenging aspect of the transition to entirely online teaching and learning?
4. How is your community college balancing the many changes that this era has brought with faculty needs?
5. What new collaborations have you seen at your community college as a result of COVID-19?
6. How are you assisting faculty in planning for the fall semester?

Appendix C

River Junction Community College Survey of Faculty

What were the most challenging aspects of the transition to entirely online teaching and learning? Mark all that apply.

- ☐ Not applicable. My classes did not transition to be entire online.
- ☐ Learning new technology
- ☐ Access to technology
- ☐ Technology fatigue
- ☐ Converting to face-to-face teaching strategies to online learning strategies
- ☐ Creating a sense of community in the online classroom
- ☐ Assisting students with technology challenges
- ☐ Other

How satisfied are you with the college's performance in regards to meeting the ever-changing needs of faculty brought about as a result of the pandemic?

☐ Very Satisfied

☐ Satisfied

☐ Neutral

☐ Dissatisfied

☐ Very Dissatisfied

Describe how you have had to change your expectations for your course, your students, and yourself.

For my students:

For myself:

Did you have to change your course materials?

☐ Yes

☐ No

Which of the following best describes how your role as a faculty member changed as a result of the pandemic?

☐ My role as a faculty member changed significantly

☐ I had to make some adjustments but did not experience significant changes

☐ My role as a faculty member did not change

Please share any additional comments concerning how the transition affected you as a faculty member.

How significantly was your mental health affected by the experience of transitioning to all online classes during the pandemic?

☐ Very significant

☐ Significant

☐ Neutral

☐ Somewhat insignificant

☐ Very insignificant

Please share any additional comments concerning the impact that transitioning to online teaching had on your mental state.

Where do you go to get resources that you need to support your teaching? Check all that apply.

☐ My department

☐ Colleagues

☐ EdTech Center

☐ Faculty Development

☐ Office of Assessment, EIO

☐ Experts in my discipline

☐ Technical Support Center

☐ Other

What new collaborations have you seen at the college as a result of COVID-19?

What changes have you made in your teaching that will continue once we are "back to normal"?

Additional Comments:

References

Adamowicz, C. (2007). On adjunct labor and community colleges. *Academe, 93*(5), 24–27.

Albers, C. (2008). Improving pedagogy through action learning and scholarship of teaching and learning. *Teaching Sociology, 36*(1), 79–86. https://doi.org/10.1177/0092055X0803600110

Alexander, B. (2020). The academic enterprise. In *The post-pandemic college*. Chronicle of Higher Education.

Arrington, N. M., & Cohen, A. (2015). Enhancing the scholarship of teaching and learning through micro-level collaboration across two disciplines. *International Journal of Teaching and Learning in Higher Education, 27*(2), 194–203.

Austin, A., & Sorcinelli, M. D. (2013). The future of faculty development: Where are we going? *New Directions for Teaching and Learning, 133,* 85–97. https://doi.org/10.1002/tl.20048

Auten, J. G., & Twigg, M. M. (2015). Teaching and learning SoTL: Preparing future faculty in a pedagogy course. *Teaching & Learning Inquiry, 3*(1), 3–13. https://doi.org/10.20343/teachlearninqu.3.1.3

Baldwin, R., & Chang, D. (2014). *Collaborating to learn, learning to collaborate.* Association of American Colleges & Universities. www.aacu.org/publications-research/periodicals/collaborating-learn-learning-collaborate

Beach, A. L., Sorcinelli, M. D., Austin, A. E., & Rivard, J. K. (2016). *Faculty development in the age of evidence: Current practices, future imperatives*. Stylus Publishing.

Becket, D., Refaei, B., & Skutar, C. (2012). A faculty learning community's reflection on implementing service-learning goals. *Journal of the Scholarship of Teaching and Learning, 12*(1), 74–86.

Bender, E., & Gray, D. (1999). *The scholarship of teaching*. Research & Creative Activity. http://www.indiana.edu/~rcapub/v22n1/p03.html

Bernstein, D., & Bass, R. (2005). The scholarship of teaching and learning. *Academe, 91*(4), 37–43.

Bolf-Beliveau, L. (2013). The scholarship of teaching and learning: Transformation and transgression. *InSight: A Journal of Scholarly Teaching, 8*, 63–68.

Bond, N. (2015). Developing a faculty learning community for non-tenure track professors. *International Journal of Higher Education, 4*(4), 1–12. https://doi.org/10.5430/ijhe.v4n4p1

Boose, D. L., & Hutchings, P. (2016). The scholarship of teaching and learning as a subversive activity. *Teaching & Learning Inquiry, 4*(1), 12. https://doi.org/10.20343/teachlearninqu.4.1.6

Boyer, E. (1990). *Scholarship reconsidered: Priorities of the professoriate*. Carnegie Foundation for the Advancement of Teaching.

Brackett, M., Cipriano, C., & Elbertson, N. (2020, December 8). *This year has taken a toll on educators. Let's make sure to support them in 2021*. EdSurge. https://www.edsurge.com/news/2020-12-08-this-year-has-taken-a-toll-on-educators-let-s-make-sure-to-support-them-in-2021

Bradshaw, L. K. (1997). *Interagency collaboration: Preconditions, progress, and pressures* [Conference presentation]. Annual Conference of the American Evaluation Association, San Diego, CA.

Brint, S., & Karabel, J. (1989). The community college and democratic ideals. *Community College Review, 17*(2), 9–19. https://doi.org/10.1177/009155218901700203

Burns, K. A. (2017). Community college faculty as pedagogical innovators: How the scholarship of teaching and learning (SoTL) stimulates innovation in the classroom. *Community College Journal of Research and Practice, 41*(3), 153–67. https://.doi.org/10.1080/10668926.2016.1168327

Cassard, A., & Sloboda, B. (2014). Leading the charge for SoTL—Embracing collaboration. *InSight: A Journal of Scholarly Teaching, 9*, 44–53. https://doi.org/10.46504/09201403ca

Center for Community College Student Engagement (CCSE). (2014). *Contingent commitments: Bringing part-time faculty into focus. A special report.* https://www.ccsse.org/docs/PTF_Special_Report.pdf

Cohen, A. M., & Brawer, F. B. (2003). *The American community college* (4th ed.). Jossey-Bass.

Colbry, S., Hurwitz, M., & Adair, R. (2014). Collaboration theory. *Journal of Leadership Education, 13*(4), 63–75. http://doi.org/10.12806/V13/14/C8

Condon, W., Iverson, E. R., Manduca, C. A., Rutz, C., & Willett, G. (2016). *Faculty development and student learning: Assessing the connections.* Indiana University Press.

Cook-Sather, A., Bahti, M., & Ntem, A. (2019). *Pedagogical partnerships: A how-to guide for faculty, students, and academic developers in higher education.* Elon University Center for Engaged Learning. https://doi.org/10.36284/celelon.oa1

Cox, M. D. (2004). Introduction to faculty learning communities. *New Directions for Teaching and Learning,* (97), 5–23. https://doi.org/10.1002/tl.129

Cox, M. D. (2016). Four positions of leadership in planning, implementing, and sustaining faculty learning community programs. *Teaching and Learning,* 85–96. https://doi.org/10.1002/tl.20212

Creswell, J. W. (2007) *Qualitative enquiry and research design: Choosing among five approaches.* SAGE Publications.

Crow, M. L. (1979). *Executive director's message.* Professional and Organizational Development Network in Higher Education.

Darling-Hammond, L., Wei, R. C., Andree, A., Richardson, N., & Orphanos, S. (2009). State of the profession: Study measures status of professional development. *Journal of Staff Development, 30*(2), 42–44.

Dewey, J. (1933). *How we think.* Heath.

Draeger, J. (2013). Why bother with the scholarship of teaching and learning? *InSight: A Journal of Scholarly Teaching, 8,* 12–19. https://.doi.org/10.46504/08201301dr

Eddy, P. L. (2010). New faculty issues: Fitting in and figuring it out. *New Directions for Community Colleges, 152,* 15–24. http://doi.org/10.1002/cc.423

Elliott, E. R., Reason, R. D., Coffman, C. R., Gangloff, E. J., Raker, J. R., Powell-Coffman, J., & Ogilvie, C. A. (2016). Improved student learning through a faculty learning community: How faculty collaboration transformed a large-enrollment course from lecture to student centered. *CBE—Life Sciences Education, 15*(2), 14. https://doi.org/10.1187/cbe.14-07-0112.

Elliott, R.W., & Oliver, D. E. (2016). Linking faculty development to community college student achievement: A mixed methods approach. *Community College Journal of Research and Practice, 40*(2), 85–99. https://doi.org/10/1080/10668926.2014.961590

Engin, M., & Atkinson, F. (2015). Faculty learning communities: A model for supporting curriculum changes in higher education. *International Journal of Teaching and Learning in Higher Education, 27*(2), 164–74.

Everett, J. B. (Fall 2011). Balancing life and work responsibilities: The advantages of teaching at community college and other 2-year colleges. *Delta Kappa Gamma Bulletin, 78*(1), 20–23.

Felten, P. (2013). Principles of good practice in SoTL. *Teaching & Learning Inquiry, 1*(1), 121–25. https://doi.org/10.2979/teachlearninqu.1.1.121

Felten, P., Kalish, A., Pingree, A., & Plank, K. M. (2007). Toward a scholarship of teaching and learning in educational development. *To improve the academy, 25*(1), 93–108. https://doi.org/10.1002/j.2334-4822.2007.tb00476.x

Fingerhut, H. (2018). Sharp partisan divisions in views of national institutions. *Pew Research Center.* http://www.people-press.org/2017/07/10/sharp-partisan-divisions-in-views-of-national-institutions/

Fisher, B. A., Repice, M. D., Dufault, C. L., Leonard, D. A., & Frey, R. F. (2014). Developing scholarly teachers through an SoTL faculty fellowship. *To Improve the Academy, 33*(2), 175–95. https://doi.org/10.1002/tia2.20011

Ford, C., & Peaslee, D. (2018). *A community college perspective on creating a SoTL scholars program.* The SoTL Advocate. https://illinoisstateuniversitysotl.wordpress.com/2018/02/26/a-community-college-perspective-on-creating-a-sotl-scholars-program/

Francis, R. (2007). Getting started with SoTL in your classroom. *International Journal for the Scholarship of Teaching and Learning, 1*(2), 6. https://doi.org/10.20429/ijsotl.2007.010220

Gaff, J. G. (1975). *Toward faculty renewal: Advances in faculty, instructional, and organizational development.* Jossey-Bass.

Gahn, S., & Twombly, S. B. (2001). Dimensions of the community college faculty labor market. *The Review of Higher Education, 24*(3), 259–82. https://doi.org/10.1353/rhe.2001.0002

Gajda, R. (2004). Utilizing collaboration theory to evaluate strategic alliances. *American Journal of Evaluation, 25*(1), 65–77. https://doi.org/10.1177/109821400402500105

Ginsberg, S. M., & Bernstein, J. L. (2011). Growing the scholarship of teaching and learning through institutional culture change. *Journal of the Scholarship of Teaching and Learning, 11*(1), 1–12.

Given, L., & Kelly, W. (2016). Collectivist information behavior: Mentoring circles as sites for knowledge creation. *Proceedings of the Association for Information Science and Technology, 53*(1), 1–10. https://doi.org/10.1002/pra2.2016.14505301059

Gordon, L., & Foutz, T. (2015). Navigating the first-year program: Exploring new waters in a faculty learning community. *International Journal of Teaching and Learning in Higher Education, 27*(1), 81–93.

Grant, M. R., & Keim, M. (2002). Faculty development in publicly supported two-year colleges. *Community College Journal of Research and Practice, 26*, 793–807. https://doi.org/10.1080/10668920290104886

Grove, J. (2017, September 21). *Online courses "more time-consuming" to prepare for, study says.* Times Higher Education. https://www.timeshighereducation.com/news/online-courses-more-time-consuming-prepare-study-says

Grubb., W. N. & Associates (1999). *Honored but invisible: An inside look at teaching in community colleges.* Routledge.

Grupp, L. L., & Little, D. (2019). Finding a fulcrum: Positioning ourselves to leverage change. *To Improve the Academy, 38*(1), 1–23. https://10.1002/tia2.20088

Hankin, J. N., & Gardner, J. N. (1996). The freshman year experience: A philosophy for higher education in the new millennium. In J. N. Hankin (Ed.), *The community college: Opportunity and access for America's first-year students* (Monograph No. 19, pp. 1–10). National Resource Center for the First-Year Experience and Students in Transition, University of South Carolina.

Hatch, T. (2005). *Into the Classroom: Developing the scholarship of teaching and learning.* Jossey-Bass.

Hodges, C., Moore, S., Lockee, B., Trust, T., & Bond, A. (2020, March 27). *The difference between emergency remote teaching and online learning.* EDUCAUSE Review. https://er.educause.edu/articles/2020/3/the-difference-between-emergency-remote-teaching-and-online-learning

Hough, B.W., Smithey, M. W., & Evertson, C. M. (2004). Using computer-mediated communication to create virtual communities of practice for intern teachers. *Journal of Technology and Teacher Education, 12*(3), 361–86.

Hutchings, P. (2003). The scholarship of teaching and learning in communication: A few words from the Carnegie academy. *Communication Education, 52*(1), 57–59. https://dci.org/10.1080/03634520302455

Hutchings, P., & Shulman, L. S. (1999). The scholarship of teaching: New elaborations, new developments. *Change, 31*(5), 10–15. https://doi.org/10.1080/00091389909604218

Jacoby, D. (2005). Part-time community college faculty and the desire for full-time tenure track positions: Results of a single institution case study. *Community College Journal of Research and Practice, 29*, 136–152. https://doi.org/10.1080/10668920490891629

Janzen, K. (2015). Encouraging scholarly teaching and learning. *College Quarterly, 18*(2), 3.

Kaufman, J. H., & Diliberty, M. K. (2021, January 15). *Teachers are not all right: How the COVID-19 pandemic is taking a toll on the nation's teachers.* RAND. https://www.rand.org/pubs/external_publications/EP68439.html

Kern, B., Mettetal, G., Dixson, M. D., & Morgan, R. K. (2015). The role of SoTL in the academy: Upon the 25th anniversary of Boyer's "scholarship reconsidered." *Journal of the Scholarship of Teaching and Learning, 15*(3), 1–14. https://doi.org/10.14434/josotl.v15i3.13623

Kerrigan, C. E. (2015). The art of collaboration. Australian Council of University Art and Design Schools.

King, J. A., & Lonnquist, M. P. (1992). *A review of writing on action research (1944–present).* Center on Organization and Restructuring of Schools. Sponsored by the Office of Educational Research and Improvement.

Latz, A. O. (2012). Flow in the community college classroom?: An autoethnographic exploration. *International Journal for the Scholarship of Teaching and Learning, 6*(2), 1–13. https://doi.org/10.20429/ijsotl.2012.060215

Levin, J. S. (2013). Understandings of community colleges in need of resuscitation: The case of community college faculty. In J. S. Levin & S. T. Kater (Eds.), *Understanding community colleges* (pp. 233–54). Routledge.

Levin, J. S., Kater, S., & Wagoner, J. L. (2006). *Community college faculty: At work in the new economy.* Palgrave Macmillan.

Levin, J. S., & Montero-Hernandez, V. (2009). *Community colleges and their students: Co-construction and organizational identity.* Palgrave Macmillan.

Lloyd, C. (2016). Leading across boundaries and silos in a single bound. *Community College Journal of Research and Practice, 40*(7), 607–14. https://doi.org/10.1080/10668926.2015.1125816

Lu, M., Todd, A. M., & Miller, M. T. (2011). Creating a supportive culture for online teaching: A case study of a faculty learning community. *Online Journal of Distance Learning Administration, 14*(3).

Marquis, E., Healey, M., & Vine, M. (2016). Fostering collaborative teaching and learning scholarship through an international writing group initiative. *Higher Education Research and Development, 35*(3), 531–44. https://doi.org/10.1080/07294360.2015.1107886

Marshall, C., & Rossman, G. B. (2016). *Designing qualitative research* (6th ed.). SAGE Publications.

McCarthy, M. (2008). The scholarship of teaching and learning in higher education: An overview. In R. Murray (Ed.), *The scholarship of teaching and learning in higher education* (pp. 6–16). McGraw Hill: Open University Press.

Michael, E. M. (2020). *Exploring community college stigma: A phenomenology of the lived experience for community college transfer students attending the University of Massachusetts Amherst.* Retrieved from ProQuest Dissertations & Theses.

Miller, S. K., Rodrigo, S., Pantoja, V., & Roen, D. (2004). Institutional models for engaging faculty in the scholarship of teaching and learning. *Teaching English in the Two-Year College, 32*(1), 30–38.

Miller-Young, J., & Yeo, M. (2015). Conceptualizing and communicating SoTL: A framework for the field. *Teaching & Learning Inquiry, 3*(2), 37–53. https://doi.org/10.20343/teachlearninqu.3.2.37

Miller-Young, J., Yeo, M., & Manarin, K. (2018). Challenges to disciplinary knowing and identity: Experiences of scholars in a SoTL development program. *International Journal for the Scholarship of Teaching and Learning, 12*(1), 6. https://doi.org/10.20429/ijsotl.2018.120103

Millward, W. T. (2020, July 27). *Online cheating isn't going away. Use it as a teachable moment for students and educators.* EdSurge. https://

www.edsurge.com/news/2020-07-27-online-cheating-isn-t-going-away
-use-it-as-a-teachable-moment-for-students-and-educators

Modern Language Association (MLA). (n.d.). A community college teaching career. Retrieved January 13, 2020, from https://www.mla.org/About-Us/Governance/Committees/Committee-Listings/Professional-Issues/Committee-on-Community-Colleges/A-Community-College-Teaching-Career

Montiel-Overall, P. (2005). Toward a theory of collaboration for teachers and librarians. *School Library Media Research*, 8, 36.

Moser, D. (2014). To lift the leaden-eyed: The historical roots of Ernest L. Boyer's "scholarship reconsidered." *American Educational History Journal*, *41*(2), 337–56. https://search-proquest-com.www2.lib.ku.edu/docview/1941331376?accountid=14556

Murray, J. P. (2001). Faculty development in publicly supported 2-year colleges. *Community College Journal of Research and Practice*, *25*, 487–502.

Murray, J. P. (2002). The current state of faculty development in two-year colleges. *New Directions for Community Colleges*, *118*, 89–98. http://doi.org/10.1002/cc.67

O'Banion, T. (1997). *A learning college for the 21st century*. American Council on Education and Oryx Press.

Ostrom, E. (1990). *Governing the commons: The evolution of institutions for collective action*. Cambridge University Press.

Patel, H., Pettitt, M., & Wilson, J. R. (2012). Factors of collaborative working: A framework for a collaboration model. *Applied Ergonomics*, *43*(1), 1–26.

Perini, M. (2014) Enhancing collaboration through the scholarship of teaching and learning. *Collaborative librarianship 6*(1), Article 8.

Poole, G., & Simmons, N. (2013). Contributions of the scholarship of teaching and learning to quality enhancement in Canada. In R. Land & G. Gordon (Eds.), *Enhancing quality in higher education: International perspectives* (pp. 118–28). Routledge.

Readman, K., & Rowe, J. (2016). Developing emerging leaders using professional learning conversations. *Higher Education Research and Development*, *35*(5), 1011–24.

Rhoads, R. A., & Valadez, J. R. (1996). *Democracy, multiculturalism, and the community college: A critical perspective*. Garland Publishing.

Richlin, L., & Cox, M. D. (2004). Developing scholarly teaching and the scholarship of teaching and learning through faculty learning communities. *New Directions for Teaching and Learning,* (97), 127–35.

Robinson-Neal, A. (2009). Exploring diversity in higher education management: History, trends, and implications for community colleges. *International Electronic Journal for Leadership in Learning, 13*(4), 1–18.

Sandell, K. L., Wigley, K., & Kovalchick, A. (2004). Developing facilitators for faculty learning communities. *New Directions for Teaching and Learning,* 51–62.

Schaffer, C. E. (2011). In their own voices: Faculty developers' perceptions of their professional identity and knowledge acquisition strategies. Widener University. ProQuest Dissertations Publishing.

Schlitz, S. A., O'Connor, M., Pang, Y., Stryker, D., Markell, S., Krupp, E., Byers, C., Jones, S. D., & Redfern, A. K. (2009). Developing a culture of assessment through a faculty learning community: A case study. *International Journal of Teaching and Learning in Higher Education, 21*(1), 133–47. https://www.learntechlib.org/p/55034/.

Schmidt, P. (2008, November 18). Studies link use of part-time instructors to lower student success. *Chronicle of Higher Education* (pp. B8–B9).

Schroeder, R. (2020, December 11). *Mental health epidemic: Dark shadow of the COVID pandemic.* Inside Higher Education. https://www.inside highered.com/digital-learning/blogs/online-trending-now/mental-health -epidemic-dark-shadow-covid-pandemic

Shannon, H. D., & Smith, R. C. (2006). A case for the community college's open access mission. *New Directions for Community Colleges,* (136), 15–21. https://doi.org/10.1002/cc.255

Shulman, L. (2000). *Fostering a scholarship of teaching and learning* [Conference presentation]. Annual Louise McBee Lecture. The University of Georgia, Athens, Georgia.

Shulman, L. (2012). "From Minsk to Pinsk: Why a scholarship of teaching and learning?" *Journal of the Scholarship of Teaching and Learning, 1*(1), 48–53.

Schuster, J. H., & Finkelstein, M. J. (2006). *The American faculty: The restructuring of academic work and careers.* Johns Hopkins University Press.

Smith, T. R., McGowan, J., Allen, A. R., Johnson, W. D., Dickson, L.A., Najee-ullah, M. A., & Peters, M. (2008). Evaluating the impact of a faculty learning community on STEM teaching and learning. *The Journal of Negro Education, 77*(3), 203–26. http://www.jstor.org/stable/25608688

Sorcinelli, M. D., Austin, A. E., Eddy, P., & Beach, A. L. (2006). *Creating the future of faculty development: Learning from the past, Understanding the present.* Jossey-Bass.

Sperling, C. B. (2003). How community colleges understand the scholarship of teaching and learning. *Community College Journal of Research and Practice, 27*(7), 593–601.

Stake, R. (2000). Case studies. In N. Denzin & Y. S. Lincoln (Eds.), *Handbook of qualitative research* (2nd edition, pp. 435–54). SAGE Publications.

Strauss, A., & Corbin, J. M. (1990). *Basics of qualitative research: Grounded theory procedures and techniques.* SAGE Publications.

Stavrakis, M. (2009). *Interaction for Design: A theoretical framework for contextual collaboration.* Doctoral thesis. https://citeseerx.ist.psu.edu/viewdoc/download?doi=10.1.1.180.4949&rep=rep1&type=pdf

Teachers College Columbia University. (n.d.) *Community college FAQs.* Columbia.edu. Retrieved January 12, 2021, from https://ccrc.tc.columbia.edu/Community-College-FAQs.html

Thomson, A., & Perry, J. (2006). Collaboration processes: Inside the black box. *Public Administration Review, 66*, 20–32. https://doi.org/10.1111/j.1540-6210.2006.00663.x

Tovar, M., Jukier, R., Ferris, J., & Cardoso, K. (2015). Overcoming pedagogical solitude: The transformative power of discipline-specific faculty learning communities. *To Improve the Academy, 34*(1), 26.

Twombly, S., & Townsend, B. K. (2008). *Community college faculty: What we know and need to know.* SAGE Publications.

U.S. Department of Education. (2017). *Community college facts at a glance.* Ed.gov. https://www2.ed.gov/about/offices/list/ovae/pi/cclo/ccfacts.html

Varagona, L., Nandan, M., Hooks, D., Porter, K. J., Maguire, M. B., & Slater-Moody, J. (2017). A model to guide the evolution of a multiprofessional group into an interprofessional team. *Journal of Faculty Development, 31*(2), 49–56.

Walls, J. K. (2016). A theoretically grounded framework for integrating the scholarship of teaching and learning. *Journal of the Scholarship of Teaching and Learning, 16*(2), 39–49.

Winkelmes, M.-A. (2011). *Analysis of several themes emerging from the 2010 POD membership survey data.* POD (Professional and Organizational Development) Network in Higher Education and Creative Commons.

Wood, D. J., & Gray, B. (1991). Toward a comprehensive theory of collaboration. *Journal of Applied Behavioral Science, 27*(2), 139.

Worthy, T. B. (2016). *Implementing the scholarship of teaching and learning in the community college office administration classroom A faculty learning community initiative.* Retrieved from ProQuest Dissertations and Theses Database.

Xu, D. (2019). Academic performance in community colleges: The influences of part-time and full-time instructors. *American Educational Research Journal, 56*(2), 368–406. https://doi.org/10.3102/0002831218796131

Yilmaz, Y., Lal, S., Tong, C., Howard, M., Bal, S., Bayer, I., Monteiro, S., & Chan, T.M. (2020). Technology-enhanced faculty development: Future trends and possibilities for health sciences education. *Medical Science Educator, 30*, 1787–96.

Yin, R. K. (2014). *Case study research: Design and methods.* SAGE Publications.

Index

About the Authors

Farrell Hoy Jenab is director of faculty development at Johnson County Community College, where she has also taught Composition and TESOL for over twenty years. Jenab received her BA from Baker University, MLS from Emporia State University, and EdD from the University of Kansas. Her research interests include the scholarship of teaching and learning (SoTL) in the community college and faculty collaboration in professional development.

Heidi L. Hallman is professor of curriculum and teaching in the Department of Curriculum and Teaching at the University of Kansas. Hallman received her BS, MS, and PhD at the University of Wisconsin–Madison. Her research interests include how prospective teachers are prepared to teach in diverse school contexts as well as professional development opportunities for teachers. Hallman is the coauthor of *Secondary English Teacher Education in the United States* (2018, Bloomsbury), winner of the National Council of English's 2018 Richard A. Meade award for research in English education.

Made in the USA
Monee, IL
10 May 2024

58282634R00085